THE CHANCE OF A LIFETIME?

George said nothing. He had turned his attention to the speaker at the front of the room. "This sounds interesting."

"I am from Seton Hall University," the speaker began, "and we have a special program that some of you might find appealing. Did you know that there is a vast need for minorities in the health professions? Did you know that in this city alone, people have to wait hours to see a doctor because there are not enough doctors on staff at the hospitals to see them?"

Sampson thought back to that day the stone fell on his foot and how the doctor with the magical X-rays had helped him heal properly.

Rameck thought of the many times he had been taken to the emergency room for various scrapes and bruises.

George thought back to his many visits to the dentist and how fascinating the whole process had been for him.

"Seton Hall University," she continued, "is dedicated to training more minority students to enter medicine, not as aides and orderlies, but as *doctors!*" She paused for effect.

George felt his heart beating faster. Could this be the chance he was looking for?

WE BEAT THE STREET
HOW A FRIENDSHIP PACT LED TO SUCCESS

DRS. SAMPSON DAVIS,

GEORGE JENKINS,

AND RAMECK HUNT

WITH SHARON M. DRAPER

PUFFIN BOOKS

PUFFIN BOOKS
Published by the Penguin Group
Penguin Young Readers Group,
345 Hudson Street, New York, New York 10014, U.S.A.
Penguin Group (Canada), 90 Eglinton Avenue East, Suite 700, Toronto, Ontario,
Canada M4P 2Y3 (a division of Pearson Penguin Canada Inc.)
Penguin Books Ltd, 80 Strand, London WC2R 0RL, England
Penguin Ireland, 25 St Stephen's Green, Dublin 2, Ireland
(a division of Penguin Books Ltd)
Penguin Group (Australia), 250 Camberwell Road, Camberwell, Victoria 3124, Australia
(a division of Pearson Australia Group Pty Ltd)
Penguin Books India Pvt Ltd, 11 Community Centre, Panchsheel Park,
New Delhi - 110 017, India
Penguin Group (NZ), Cnr Airborne and Rosedale Roads, Albany, Auckland 1310,
New Zealand (a division of Pearson New Zealand Ltd)
Penguin Books (South Africa) (Pty) Ltd, 24 Sturdee Avenue,
Rosebank, Johannesburg 2196, South Africa

Registered Offices: Penguin Books Ltd, 80 Strand, London WC2R 0RL, England

First published in the United States of America by Dutton Children's Books,
a division of Penguin Young Readers Group, 2005
Published by Puffin Books, a division of Penguin Young Readers Group, 2006

30 29 28 27 26 25 24

Puffin Books ISBN 0-14-240627-9

Printed in the United States of America

Uncle T.J., I will miss you;
you are a great man!

—SAMPSON DAVIS, M.D.

Ellen Bradley—
Ma, this one's for you too!

—RAMECK HUNT, M.D.

For Annette and Jackie.
There is always hope.
I believe in you.

—SHARON DRAPER

CONTENTS

WE BEAT THE STREET

THIS IS A TRUE STORY. We are real people. We started out as kids in the toughest neighborhoods of Newark, New Jersey, and today we are doctors. We had to fight drugs and crime and hopelessness. We had to overcome obstacles like poverty and apathy and violence in our community. Individually we probably would not have succeeded, but together, we were able to make it through high school, college, and medical school.

We are Dr. Rameck Hunt, Dr. Sampson Davis, and Dr. George Jenkins. We call ourselves The Three Doctors. We now work in the same community where we grew up, trying to help the people in our neighborhoods.

We never thought our story was anything special. It wasn't until after we finished medical school that the public showed us what a remarkable journey we had made. In retrospect, it's probably best that it happened that way. If we had thought about how daunting the task was that we were undertaking, we probably never would have even tried.

In these pages we want to show the power of friendship and of positive peer pressure. We also want to show the necessity for strong role models in the lives of young people. The three of us suffered because we didn't have many, and we hope to offer young people today three strong, positive role models they can depend on.

Don't get us wrong—we made lots of mistakes. We often made foolish decisions, sometimes got involved in dangerous situations, and frequently suffered the consequences of impulsive behavior. But we weren't bad kids—just kids in need of focus and direction.

We want to show that obstacles can be overcome and how struggles can lead to success. We hope that by reading our story, young people can avoid some of the mistakes we made and perhaps can be inspired to reach for dreams of their own.

Many of the names of the real people who lived and died in our neighborhoods have been changed in this book to protect their privacy. But their stories are important and need to be shared.

We hope that our story will add a beacon of hope to young people in particular and to society in general. Anyone with a dream can succeed and with that success return to where it all started and make the world just a little better.

CHAPTER ONE

"YOU DON'T HAVE TO CUT MY FOOT OFF, DO YOU?"

SAMPSON, AGE 6 "I'm going with you," six-year-old Sampson Davis boldly told his big brother, Andre. Sampson, with honey-gold skin; large eyes with long lashes; and dark, curly hair, stood with his feet spread apart and his arms folded across his chest, daring his brother to challenge him. He had learned early to look and act tough, especially with the older boys his brother hung around with.

"No, man. You too little. You be crampin' my style," Andre replied.

"I don't care. I'm goin' anyway. Besides, Moms said you gotta watch me today," Sampson said, knowing that when their mother said something, she meant business. Both boys knew better than to disobey their mother. She did her best to keep her children in line and had been known to use both broom and belt on them when they broke her rules.

Sampson also knew his brother hated for him to tag along with the bigger boys. Andre was ten and had his own set of friends from the neighborhood.

"Well, just keep your mouth shut, and don't do nothin' stupid," Andre warned. "Me and my boys got business to take care of." He swaggered a little, making sure his little brother noticed. Sampson grinned and ran quickly to join them on the sidewalk.

Sampson and Andre and his friends liked to pretend to be tough, but not all of it was pretending. Kids learned early in the area around the Dayton Street Projects that walking with an air of being in control was often necessary for survival.

"You hear Peewee got beat up last night?" Andre asked his friend Leslie as they walked down the street.

"Yeah, man, he had it comin' to him. You don't take money from the Bomb and not get tightened up. He's lucky he ain't dead."

Sampson listened carefully, saying nothing, but taking it all in—confident he could handle the knowledge of activities of boys much older than he. He didn't think it was unusual at all to be discussing fights and drug deals and muggings. That's just how the world around him functioned. There was no alternative to compare it to. His stomach sometimes tightened with a mixture of fear and excitement, but he didn't let the older boys know it.

The group walked down Dayton Street in Newark, New Jersey, that summer afternoon, laughing, cussing, and spitting on the sidewalk just to show this little bit of turf belonged to them. They had no particular destination in mind and ended up in a small, grassy park not far from the projects. As Sampson walked with the older boys, he gloried in the warmth of the lazy afternoon sun.

"Look at how they keep this place," Andre said with disgust, his voice full of fifth-grade authority. The park was filled with broken glass, balled-up potato-chip bags, beer bottles, and other bits of trash. "Trash bins all bent up and full of garbage—no wonder nobody comes here."

"Yeah, look at this mess," Sampson said, sounding like a smaller version of his big brother. "How somebody 'sposed to sit on these park benches—all falling over and broke." The concrete frames, tilted and no longer braced in the dirt, wobbled easily when the boys tried to set them straight. The green wooden slats that made up the benches' seats and backs lay strewn on the grass.

"Let's fix the benches!" one of Andre's friends said suddenly. "We'll be like construction workers!"

"How we gonna do that?" Sampson asked, intrigued at the game.

"Easy, man," Andre replied enthusiastically. "We got the parts. All we gotta do is put them back together."

The boys picked up some of the trash, then began to stack the green wooden slats so they could attempt to re-assemble one of the benches.

Andre grabbed a heavy concrete slab and lifted it with a great deal of difficulty. He called out to his little brother, "Yo, Sampson, hold this straight, man."

The stone slab was a lot heavier than Sampson thought it would be as he tried to steady it. He trembled a little from the weight but refused to give up. He felt like it was him against this piece of rock, and he was determined to be stronger than concrete that day. He held it as straight as he could, hoping they would get the wood lined up quickly.

"You making it wiggle, Sampson!"

"No, I'm not! I got it!" Sampson responded through gritted teeth. The slab tilted even more. Sweat ran from Sampson's head. His hands were wet with perspiration, which made the piece of concrete harder to hold.

"Come on, man, hold on!" Andre said. "We doing the hard work—all you got to do is sit there and hold it steady."

Sampson had no chance to answer, for at that moment all two hundred pounds of the concrete slab fell forward and landed directly on his foot. At first he didn't cry out, but then the pain grew from a dull surprise to fiery intensity. "My foot!" he screamed. He clenched his face so that the older boys could not see his tears, but finally he just didn't care. He let the tears and screams escape. Dark red blood stained his sneaker and the dusty dirt beneath it. That's when he knew it was bad.

"Moms is gonna kill me!" Andre cried with fear and worry. "Help me get this thing off his foot!" he called to his friends. It took four fifth-graders to lift the concrete off Sampson's crushed foot.

Sampson looked up at his big brother and at the bright summer sky that seemed so far above him. He felt dizzy. "It hurts, Andre," he said softly.

"Tough it up, man. It's just a little bruise. We gonna get you home now," Andre said, his voice alternating between terror and toughness. He and Leslie pulled Sampson up from the ground. "Can you walk, man?"

Sampson put one foot down, then tried the other. He cringed, cried out, then slumped back against his brother. "I can't," he said, shaking his head. Sampson took several deep breaths. Sweat poured off his face.

Andre looked at Leslie. The rest of the boys had somehow disappeared. "We gotta carry him, man." Leslie nodded, and the two of them hoisted the smaller boy between them and carried him home, down the same street, which now seemed even hotter.

They got to the house, looked around for Moms, then gently set Sampson down on the couch. Leslie left quickly, knowing to get out of the way of anybody's angry mother. Sampson placed his injured foot on the sofa pillow. Blood seeped through and stained it dark red.

"We gotta tell Moms," Sampson declared. "I can't hide this blood very long."

"She gonna kill us both," Andre said.

"You first," Sampson teased, even though the pain was beginning to intensify now that he was sitting still.

Their mother, Ruthener Davis, came down the steps then, carrying a broom to sweep the living room. She took one glance at the boys, the blood, and the guilty expressions on their faces and lit into Andre with the broom. "I told you to keep an eye on your brother!" she yelled as the broomstick connected with his butt—at least when she could catch him. "What were you doing to almost squash his foot? Have you lost your mind?" She screamed and raged, chasing Andre with the broom. Sampson said nothing, trying not to let on how much it hurt.

Andre finally ran upstairs, and Moms took a closer look at Sampson's foot. "And you," she said to him, "what on earth were you thinking? You should know better. We gotta get you to the doctor, boy, before you bleed to death all over my sofa. Lord have mercy, what you all gonna get into next?"

At the emergency room of Beth Israel Hospital, dozens of people sat in chairs in the small waiting room. Even though his foot throbbed like lightning and thunder, Sampson was fascinated with the place—the energetic and constantly moving nurses; the doctors, who seemed so distant and self-assured; the people on the chairs, some patient and hopeful, some obviously in distress.

Since his foot was still bleeding and had begun to swell, Sampson was called back to the examination room sooner than some of the others who had lesser injuries or illnesses. A tall doctor in a white coat pulled back the thin curtain and walked boldly into the tiny cubicle. He glanced at the chart and looked directly at Sampson's bloody foot.

"Can you fix his foot, doctor?" Sampson's mother asked immediately.

"We're going to do our best, ma'am. Let's see what we have here."

The doctor took a stethoscope from around his neck and listened to Sampson's heart and lungs. He looked in his mouth and ears with a small flashlight. Sampson thought that was pretty stupid—it was clear that this doctor didn't know what he was doing. But he was in too much pain to say anything.

"How'd you hurt your foot, son?" the doctor asked gently.

Not sure whether he was more afraid of his mother, who would still probably punish him, or this doctor, who obviously didn't know the difference between a chest and a foot, Sampson mumbled, "A rock fell on it while I was playing."

"Pretty big rock," the doctor replied. Sampson said nothing, but watched, fascinated, as the doctor carefully removed his shoe and sock, both sticky with blood. His foot looked like something from a monster movie—swollen and bloody.

The doctor picked up his leg, gently touched the areas that hurt the most, then placed it back on the examining table. "I'm pretty sure you've got a broken foot, son. You won't be running any races or going to the swimming pool anytime soon."

"You mean he's gonna be laid up all summer?" Sampson's mother asked with a sigh.

"He'll be out of the cast and as good as new by the time school starts," the doctor replied with a smile.

Dismayed at the thought of missing all the fun and freedom of summer, Sampson secretly cursed the concrete and his foot. "So what you gonna do?" Sampson asked the doctor.

"First we get an X-ray. That means we take a picture of the bones in your foot and see exactly where it is broken. I'll let you see the picture."

"For real? You can see the inside of my foot?"

"Yes. You can see your bones and soft muscle tissue with this kind of picture."

"Cool," Sampson replied, still very much in pain, but fascinated with the process. An attendant took him down to the X-ray room, where they laid him on another table. The room was darkened, and a large machine, which whirred softly, moved above his foot. Sampson felt nothing but was amazed at the magic that seemed to surround him.

When he was returned to the examining room, he waited patiently for the doctor to come back with the pictures. The doctor came in, smiled, and said, "You've managed to break several bones in your foot, my young friend. You want to see?"

Sampson watched as the doctor placed the films of his foot on a lighted panel on the wall. The inside of a small foot appeared, with the bones of five toes, five longer bones in segments, and several other bony structures he couldn't identify. He could clearly see cracks that didn't seem to belong there.

"Everything is so even and neat," Sampson said, marveling at the picture. "Except for the broken part."

The doctor, seemingly impressed by the boy's observation, pointed out the bones of the foot and even named them for him. Sampson could have looked at the films for hours, but the doctor was busy and had other patients to see. He clicked off the screen, and the room returned to normal.

"How do you fix something like that?" Sampson asked the doctor. "You don't have to cut my foot off, do you?"

The doctor laughed. "No, son. We will have to position your foot so that the bones grow back together correctly. Then, to make sure that the foot stays still and the bones grow right, we will put your foot in a cast."

Sampson had seen casts on people before. He had always secretly wanted one because kids with casts got lots of attention, and other kids got to write on them. "Cool," he said to the doctor. "I want the light blue one."

When Sampson arrived back home, instead of being punished, he ended up being the center of attention. He got to stay in his mother's room and watch her television. But best of all, he was served dinner every night, and he didn't have to do any chores. As the summer progressed, the pain subsided; the cast got dirty; and by the time school started in the fall, the cast was off; and he was back running with his friends. He forgot about the adventure in the emergency room that summer. Almost.

HANGING TOUGH

You learned to grow up quickly around the Dayton Street Projects, where I lived when I was a boy. It was necessary to prove how tough you were, especially in the eyes of older boys. Hanging out with the older boys was always cool, and I loved being a part of that group, even though it sometimes got me in trouble.

Kids often make mistakes and do things that are sometimes foolish or dangerous. Most of the time, just like me, they don't plan to get involved in something they shouldn't—it just happens. My mother, even though she acted like she was very angry at us, was probably really worried that I was seriously injured. When I got home from the hospital, I was treated like a little prince, with extra privileges and freedom from chores.

Some say there is a reason for everything. Breaking my foot was the first time I had the opportunity for an in-depth encounter with a doctor. Of course, I couldn't know it at the time, but that experience planted the seeds of interest in emergency medicine. Years later, when I became a doctor, those seeds grew and blossomed.

And you know what? I am now working as a doctor in the neighborhood where I grew up. I am an emergency medicine physician at the same hospital where my broken foot was treated. ■

CHAPTER TWO

"OH, MAN, YOU'RE IN TROUBLE AGAIN!"

RAMECK, AGE 9 Nine-year-old Rameck Hunt was in trouble again. For the third time that week, he sat in the "Oh-man-you-in-trouble-now" chair in the principal's office and waited for the nun to come out and yell at him once more.

"Rameck, what have you done this time?" she asked as she ushered him into a room so small he felt like he couldn't breathe. The tall nun, dressed all in black, never smiled.

"It wasn't my fault, Sister. I finished my work, and I just wanted to see if I threw my pencil up to the ceiling real hard, if it would stick there. So I kept tossing it up. I almost made it, too," he added proudly. "Then a couple of the other kids saw what I was doing and started copying me, so the teacher threw me out of class. Again." After saying it, Rameck knew his explanation sounded dumb. He picked at a loose thread on his uniform.

"Of course it was your fault," the nun replied sharply. "Someone could have been seriously hurt when the pencils landed."

Rameck wanted to say that he doubted a falling pencil could kill anybody, but he figured he was in enough trouble already. He sighed and wished once more that his mother had not transferred him from public school to this Catholic school, where the rules were strict, and the academic work was easy. In a way he liked telling people he went to Catholic school, because to the kids in the neighborhood, it meant your family had a little money. But the reality of going to the school every day was not the same as boasting to your friends.

"Why didn't you just do your arithmetic like the rest of your class?" the principal asked. "There were one hundred problems on your class work assignment."

"I finished it. It was easy," Rameck told her. "I learned multiplication and division at my old school."

It was the principal's turn to sigh. "Rameck, little boys who cause constant disruptions in class never grow up to be successful people. You must learn self-control."

"I'm trying, Sister," Rameck said, "but I get bored, and my

"BOYS WHO CAUSE CONSTANT DISRUPTIONS IN CLASS NEVER GROW UP TO BE SUCCESSFUL PEOPLE. YOU MUST LEARN SELF-CONTROL."

mind gets to thinking about stuff, and then I'm in trouble again."

The principal cleared her throat. "Your teacher and I think that perhaps you should be tested for special education."

"What's special education?" Rameck asked. He rarely got to feel special at school these days. Perhaps this was something really cool.

"It's a classroom where the pace is slower, the classes are smaller, and you would not have the distractions of so many academic and social challenges," the principal replied.

Rameck frowned. "I know what you're really saying. But I'm not slow, Sister. I like doing the work in class. And I like the kids here. I even like the school. Really." He looked at her with honest confusion. "I can't help it if I keep getting in trouble!"

"I will discuss this with your mother. We feel it might be for the best," the principal said. "Get back to class now, and try to behave." The principal looked at him through the glasses perched on her nose. "Oh, and Rameck . . ."

"Yes, ma'am," the boy replied as he turned to leave.

"Tell your mother that her tuition payment is due on Friday."

Rameck rolled his eyes and stomped out of her office. The principal made him feel angry and stupid. He balled up his fist, knocked over the chair reserved for kids in trouble, and stormed into the hall.

The hallway, with its scuffed floors and tall windows covered with wire, loomed ahead of him, empty and silent. All the classroom doors were closed, but Rameck could hear sounds coming from each one as he passed by—the singsong chant of first-graders, the noisy disruption of the sixth-graders. Rameck, full of pent-up anger and frustration, took a deep breath. At the far end of the hall a sixth-grade boy Rameck knew only as Meatball came out of his classroom with a bathroom pass. Meatball was a bully and had been pushing Rameck around at lunchtime.

In public school, Rameck had learned to fight to solve his problems. But in this Catholic school, even though he felt out of place, Rameck had gradually learned to solve his problems through peaceful means. But sometimes a fight was unavoidable. The boy walked toward him, and Rameck imagined himself in a cowboy movie. He would be the cool cowboy with the black hat, the fast horse, and the silver bullets in his gun. Just the two of them, heading toward each other down the dusty street, waiting for the showdown.

Meatball, much larger and stronger-looking than Rameck, glared at him as the two got closer. "Yo' mama's on welfare!" the boy hissed as he passed. Rameck was sure that the kid didn't even know his mother, but he wasn't going to let this dude talk about her.

Rameck had had enough. He made a fist and punched Meatball in the stomach. "Don't you be talking about my mama!" he growled as he hit the boy again. Rameck, glad to have an excuse to release some of his frustration, pulled Meatball down on the floor, and the two rolled around in the empty hallway for several minutes, exchanging fierce punches and pent-up anger.

A classroom door opened then, and both boys, almost on cue, jumped up, dusted off their wrinkled and torn uniforms, and headed off in opposite directions. Rameck somehow felt better. He had no idea how the other boy felt, but he had a feeling that he wouldn't be picking on Rameck anymore.

Basically, Rameck liked most of the students at this school. They came from a wide background of families and cultures, and as his first exposure to people different from himself, Rameck thought it was pretty cool. But he'd never tell that to the dour nun in the principal's office.

When Rameck got home that afternoon, his mother was asleep. He thought she looked beautiful as she lay there. In fact, she was so pretty she could be Miss America. Of course, he had never seen a black Miss America, but he figured there's always a first time.

He didn't wake her, but left and headed for his grandmother's house, a few blocks away. "Hey, Ma," he called to her as he walked into her warm kitchen, which smelled of fried chicken. All of her children and grandchildren simply called her Ma.

"How you doin', boy?" His grandmother gave him a big hug. "You hungry?"

Rameck nodded and grabbed an apple from the kitchen table. "All the time!"

"How was school, Rameck?" his grandmother asked as she fixed him a plate.

"I don't know. Those nuns be trippin'! They always yelling at me. I want to go back to my old school." Rameck conveniently left out the part about the fight.

"Your mother put you in that school so you could get a better education, boy. Don't mess that up," his grandmother warned.

"But I already know the stuff they be doing in class, Ma. And the principal said she was gonna put me in special education because I can't behave."

"But you're so smart," his grandmother said. "Weren't you in a gifted and talented after-school program last year?"

Rameck nodded, then pounded the table with his fist. Forks and spoons flew to the floor. "This ain't fair, Ma."

"It doesn't make sense that this school thinks you need to be in special ed," his grandmother mused.

"Tell me about it," Rameck said glumly as he ate his dinner.

"Maybe I'll talk to your mama, and we can get you out of there. There's no way she's gonna let them put you in classes for slow children."

"If I go back to public school, I can go back to that program," Rameck said hopefully. "The lady who runs it, Mrs. Hatt, told me I was smart—and cute, too!" Rameck grinned, large dimples showing on his round brown face.

Ma laughed and pinched Rameck's cheek. "We're gonna see what we can do to get you out of that school and back to a place where you can do well. We expect a lot from you, you know that, boy?"

"Yes, ma'am," Rameck replied. He hated being pushed, but at the same time he loved the high expectations his family set for him.

"Your mama go to work today?" his grandmother then asked.

Rameck nodded. "I guess. She was 'sleep when I got home. She works pretty hard. I think she gets paid tomorrow."

"Your mama loves you. You know that, don't you? She wants the best for you. But sometimes life gets bigger than she is," his grandmother told him. "You'll understand that when you get grown."

"I know she loves me," Rameck replied. "Last year when we went to Disney World, everybody on the block was hatin' me. That was too cool!" His smile faded a little. "But sometimes I just wish . . ."

"I know what you wish, and wishing ain't gonna change nothing! Can't nobody help you but yourself! You do what you got to do, and make your life something we all can be proud of." Ma always took the "tough love" stance with Rameck— giving him support but never babying him.

"Yes, ma'am," Rameck replied obediently. But he had no idea how to reach his grandmother's expectations. He couldn't even figure out how to deal with the next day.

SCHOOL PROBLEMS

The third and fourth grades were challenging for me. I came from a public school system where the culture was very different. The jokes were more hurtful, and problems were solved with your fist. At the Catholic school I attended when I was eight and nine years old, problems were solved by talking them out. It took me some time to get used to this more peaceful approach, but once I did, I actually liked it. Another reason I grew to like the school was that, in a way, going to a Catholic school meant your family had a little money, so it made me feel good to tell other kids in the neighborhood where I went to school. There was so much around me that shouted "poor" or "dysfunctional" that going to a Catholic school combated that negativity a little.

But because of the threat of special education, and because funding for the private school finally became a difficulty, I ended up back in public school. I had to reacquaint myself with my old culture, which was challenging as well as discouraging. The transition was awkward for me because I had stopped handling my problems with fighting.

Schoolwork was never a problem for me. Classes were easy, and learning was fun. But since I was always the type that needed my mind stimulated constantly, and because I had a little trouble with self-control, I was always into something. It took me many years to gain self-control. Controlling your behavior is just as important as what you learn in school. Good grades mean nothing if you're always in the principal's office. It took me a while to figure that out. ∎

CHAPTER THREE

"ISN'T THAT SCHOOL IN THE GHETTO?"

GEORGE, AGE 8 "Quit throwin' bottles in the street, man," eight-year-old George Jenkins yelled to his older brother, Garland.

"You can't make me," his brother taunted back. He picked up a green wine bottle he found in the gutter and tossed it onto the hard concrete of Muhammad Ali Avenue in Newark, New Jersey. It shattered into dozens of glistening fragments that shimmered in the sunlight.

"Suppose a car runs over the glass and gets a flat tire," George asked. Garland was almost ten, and George didn't think he acted his age.

"Too bad for them," Garland said as he tossed another bottle. "Hey, now, look at that one—two bounces and a smash!"

He cheered as the brown beer bottle exploded and shattered.

"Hey, man, I'm outta here. I ain't gonna be late because of you." George glared at his brother before hurrying off in the direction of Louise A. Spencer Elementary School. Garland, he noticed, headed off in the other direction, once again skipping classes for the day.

George loved school. Even though it was located in what was described as the "inner city," it was relatively new and neat and clean. His third-grade teacher, Miss Viola Johnson, was a tiny ball of energy with a high-pitched voice and the same honey-colored skin as George's mother. There was no doubt as to her power and authority in that classroom. Miss Johnson made every day an adventure, and George hated to miss school, even on days when he was sick.

George slid quietly into the room, only a couple of minutes late, and grinned at Miss Johnson, who noticed his tardiness but said nothing.

"Today," she began, "we're going to continue talking about the writer named Shakespeare. How long ago did he live?" she asked the class.

"Four hundred years ago!" they responded immediately.

"How many plays did he write?"

"Thirty-seven!"

George had no idea that Shakespeare was not usually taught in third grade. Miss Johnson simply offered it, and George, as well as the rest of his class, absorbed it.

"What was so cool about this Shakespeare dude, Miss Johnson?" a boy named Ritchie wanted to know. George wished he just would shut up so Miss Johnson could talk.

"Well, for one thing, Shakespeare wore an earring," Miss Johnson offered.

"For real? Real gold?" Ritchie seemed to be impressed.

"Here's another interesting fact," Miss Johnson said. "In order to seek his fortune as an actor and a writer, Shakespeare ran away from home shortly after he got married, leaving his wife and three children to make it without him," Miss Johnson explained.

"Sounds like yo' daddy!" Ritchie yelled to the boy sitting next to him. Both of them cracked up with laughter.

Every Tuesday she told them all about Shakespeare's time—about kings and castles, as well as about the rats and fleas that lived in the straw that most people used for bedding. "Did you know that during Shakespeare's time almost a third of the people who lived in London died one year from something called the Black Plague?" she asked the class.

"Why?" George asked.

"There were very few doctors at that time, and they didn't know what we know today about cleanliness and sanitation. Most people just threw their garbage out the window every morning, as well as the contents of their chamber pots. That's what they used at night. Toilets had not been invented yet."

"Yuk!" the class responded.

The class listened, fascinated and entranced with her stories, which taught them history, literature, math, and science without them

"IT'S HARD TO FIT IN WITH YOUR BOYS IF YOUR GRADES ARE TOO GOOD."

even being aware of it. She passed out a children's version of *Hamlet*, full of pictures and explanations, and let them read the play and act out the fight scenes.

Every day went quickly in Miss Johnson's class, but she often stayed after school with them to make cookies or build projects. She even took them into New York City sometimes to let them see live plays on Broadway or to hear orchestra concerts at Lincoln Center. George loved to listen to the drums and horns and violins as they mixed up together in that huge concert hall.

When her students formed the Shakespeare Club, Miss Johnson even helped them get sweaters. They were deep burgundy with the name of the club embroidered on the pocket. George and his classmates wore them proudly to a concert one afternoon.

During the intermission, a woman wearing too much perfume and a mink coat, even though it was the middle of spring, walked up to George and said, "What lovely sweaters you and your classmates are wearing."

"Thank you, ma'am," George said with a grin, touching the careful embroidery.

"What private school do you children attend?" the woman asked.

Miss Johnson walked over to the woman and said proudly, "These are students from Louise Spencer Elementary, a public school in the Central Ward."

"But they're so well behaved," the woman said with surprise. "Isn't that school in the ghetto?"

Miss Johnson gave the woman a look that could have

melted that mink coat and led her students away. George looked back at the woman with hurt and confusion. He wished he could have tripped the smelly old lady.

On the way back home from this trip, George, always the quiet kid, sat alone on the bus seat. "Mind if I sit next to you, George?" someone asked.

He looked up, pulled his long legs out of the aisle, and smiled at her. "Sure, Miss Johnson."

"Did that woman upset you?" she asked.

George shrugged. "I don't know. She smelled like mothballs."

"There will always be people like that, you know," Miss Johnson explained.

"Yeah, I know."

"And you can either let them hold you back, or you can ignore them and go on and do your thing."

"Yeah, I know." George didn't want to admit how much the woman's words had hurt. He changed the subject. "That was a good concert, Miss Johnson. I think it's really cool that you take us to stuff like this."

"Perhaps when you go to college you can learn to write symphonies or plays of your own," she said.

"College? I never even thought about it." To George, the idea of college seemed like something foreign and vague, like going to China or the moon.

"Of course you'll go to college. You're one of the smartest children in my class." Miss Johnson spoke with certainty. "I have high hopes and great expectations for you, George."

"Maybe you do, but some kids think it ain't cool to be too smart, you know," George told her.

"That's the dumbest thing I ever heard!" Miss Johnson said loudly. The other kids on the bus looked up to see what had upset her.

"You don't understand," George said quietly. "It's hard to fit in with your boys if your grades are too good."

"Nonsense!" Miss Johnson replied. "You don't really believe that."

George grinned at her. "Yeah, I guess you're right. I guess I really don't care what they think of me."

"College is cool, George. If you can fit in there, you've got it made."

"Doesn't it take a long time?" George asked, chewing on his lip. He felt a combination of excitement and wonder.

"It takes four years to complete the first part of college," she explained. "At the end of that time, you'll be four years older whether you go to college or not, so you might as well go and get as much knowledge in your head as you can."

George looked out of the bus window and thought about what she had said. As the field-trip bus got closer to his neighborhood in Newark, he looked at the tall, poverty-ridden, high-rise apartments like the one he lived in; the boarded-up and defeated stores; and the trash all over the streets.

"I don't know how," he said quietly, helpless in his lack of knowledge.

Miss Johnson didn't laugh, however. She just smiled and said, "It's not very hard. Just do your best, keep your nose out of trouble, and one day the doors will open for you."

For the first time, George could see a glimpse of light, a spark of hope and possibility. College. What a cool idea.

INFLUENTIAL TEACHERS

It's amazing how much of a positive effect one teacher can have on the life of a student. Miss Johnson was the most influential person in my life when I was in grade school. Thanks to her, I never believed my situation was hopeless. Thanks to her, I learned to dream beyond my environment. Thanks to her, I was able to see a glimpse of the future. She inspired me, encouraged me, and motivated me. She made learning fun and made opportunities possible. The field trips she took us on opened my eyes to a world I didn't even know existed.

She brainwashed our class with positive messages, which made it easy to deal with the negativity in our environment. She believed in all of us, and because of her, I learned to believe in myself.

When I got older and times got tough, lessons I learned from Miss Johnson in those early years helped me to see that difficulties are only temporary. Her inspiration helped me to stay focused on accomplishing my goals. Because of her encouragement when I needed it, I now hope that I am a positive role model and inspiration to others. I do all that I can to help young people to believe in themselves and strive toward a positive future. ■

CHAPTER FOUR

"WE'RE GONNA JACK US SOME ICEES FROM JACK'S!"

SAMPSON, AGE 8 "Wanna play some sponge ball?" Sampson yelled to his best friends, Noody and Will.

"Let's get it on!" Noody shouted back. "I got a bat. You got a ball?"

"Yeah, I found one in the lot by your building," Sampson said.

"That musta been the one I lost," Noody replied with a grin. Noody was a couple of years younger than Sampson and Will, but he was so good in baseball they loved having him around. He was skinny, with pecan-brown skin and a constant smile.

"You ain't got no dollar to buy no sponge ball, man. You trippin'!" Will said with a laugh as the three friends headed to the barely paved parking lot of the Dayton Street Projects, which was filled with weeds, sparse patches of grass, broken glass, and all kinds of debris. The three boys played baseball for hours in that lot during hot summer days, with the hopes of one day going pro—playing for a major league team. Sampson knew it was a long shot, but he felt his talents exceeded those of any kid his age, and he had big dreams. It seemed to him that baseball might be his only escape from the ghetto.

Sampson lived right across the street from the Dayton Street Projects. His house was nothing much, but he and his friends jokingly called it "the penthouse of the projects." The Dayton Street Project, Building 6, was an eight-story building with broken elevators, abandoned apartments, and hallways that reeked with urine. Broken lightbulbs decorated the halls, so the halls were always dark, even in the daytime. Residents and visitors crept cautiously to their destinations, hoping no one would attack them on a trip up the littered stairs to one of the apartments.

Drug dealers and buyers constantly hung out in the stair-wells of the apartments, but they were so commonplace that the boys had learned to ignore them and play games in their shadow.

The three boys took turns with the positions—one would pitch, aiming for a box etched in chalk on the brick wall of the building; one would play the outfield; and the third would bat. It wasn't major league, but it filled up a summer after-noon.

"You missed that one by a mile!" Sampson laughed as Will struck out during his turn at bat.

"That's 'cause you can't pitch!" Noody retorted.

Their laughter was interrupted by an angry-looking man with a deep red scar across his cheek. He ran directly toward Sampson. "Give me that bat!" the man demanded viciously. Noody and Will huddled close to Sampson, ready to back him up if necessary. The three were tight.

Sampson knew better than to refuse, so without a word he let the man, a neighborhood drug dealer known as the Bomb, snatch his bat. The Bomb, a street legend, marched over to the stairwell, cursed loudly at another man huddled there, and then proceeded to beat the man brutally with Sampson's bat. The man in the stairwell, who probably had run out of money before he ran out of his need for drugs, cried out with fear and pain and then was silent.

The Bomb emerged from the stairwell, breathing hard, but looking fiercely satisfied. He tossed the bat back to Sampson, who did not catch it, but let it fall to the ground. "Thanks, kid," the Bomb said. "Finish your game now." He disappeared down the street.

The three boys, who somehow had lost their desire to play ball, headed down Dayton Street. They left the bat where it lay. They had seen it all before, and they knew they would see similar events again. It was the norm in the projects.

DRUG DEALERS AND BUYERS WERE SO COMMONPLACE THAT THE BOYS HAD LEARNED TO IGNORE THEM AND PLAY GAMES IN THEIR SHADOW.

Will spoke first. "I guess that's just the way it is, man." They all knew what he meant.

"I don't care," Sampson said. "I ain't never gonna do no drugs."

"What about sellin' them?" Will asked.

"Easy money," Noody observed.

"All I know is I ain't never letting nobody beat me upside my head with no bat!" Sampson asserted. The three boys, already numb to the chaos that surrounded them, knew that staying out of trouble was a lot harder than just talking about it.

"It must be ninety degrees out here, man," Sampson said as they walked down Dayton Street and away from the parking lot.

"Sponge ball always makes me thirsty," Noody said, wiping the sweat from his forehead.

"I wish I had an Icee," Will said, licking his lips.

"Extra large," Sampson added. "Frosty and cold."

"Let's go to Jack's and get us some Icees!" Will, who was always cracking jokes, suggested. Jack's, the corner store that sold everything from beer to bubble gum, was a familiar hangout.

"We ain't got no money, man," Noody reminded them.

"I got an idea," Sampson said. "Will, you be the lookout, and make sure the way is clear. Me and Noody will go in, get the Icees, and put them in our shorts. It'll be easy!" Since the boys were often without money, this was not the first time they had targeted a local store for a free snack.

"We gonna jack us some Icees from Jack's!" Will chanted as the three friends ran down the street to the little store.

Sitting near the front of the store were a few neighborhood bums, always begging for a quarter to help them with their next high. Inside, the store smelled of candy and baloney and wine. Sampson loved this little store, and the owner, Jack, a large Hispanic man, would often give them pieces of candy when he was in a good mood. Today, however, the weather was oppressively hot, and Jack sat near the cash register, fanning himself. The Icee freezer was on the other side of the store, near the bread and the dog food. The three boys entered the store, not with their usual noise and cheerful hellos, but silently, looking around and checking behind them as if they were professional thieves. Several customers were in the store—folks who had stopped by to pick up a few necessary groceries or goodies before heading home.

Jack said nothing and continued to fan himself, pretending to ignore the boys. Will stood by the door as planned, whistling. Sampson and Noody tiptoed to the Icee freezer and quickly filled two extra-large cups of the cold, frosty drinks. Each boy then took a cup and stuffed it inside the front of his shorts. Sampson gasped as the cold cup touched his body—he never knew there could be such freezing pain.

Walking slowly and awkwardly, Sampson and Noody moved toward the door, sure they had succeeded in a difficult but well-planned robbery. The bulge from the Icees was ridiculously noticeable through the children's summer shorts, but they were confident in their success. Just as they reached the door, Sampson felt a thick hand on the back of his T-shirt. He looked back and saw Jack, large and looming and very angry, grab Noody as well. Will, who was supposed to have been their lookout, saw what was happening and disappeared down the street in an instant.

Jack, screaming and cursing at them in both English and Spanish, dragged Sampson and Noody from the front door, where escape had been only seconds away, to the back of the store. The Icee fell out of Sampson's clothes onto the wooden floor of Jack's store.

Sampson screamed, "I was gonna pay for that, Jack! Come on, you know me. I come in here all the time!"

Jack ignored him and continued to drag the two boys through a storage room and out the backdoor, to an area that Sampson had never seen before. Sampson and Noody screamed and prayed for their lives. They had both heard horror stories about how Jack would chop the hands off of people who stole from his store.

There was a fenced-in area outside. Behind that fence stood the two biggest German shepherd dogs that Sampson had ever seen. The dogs barked loudly and ferociously at all the screaming and commotion in front of them. Their teeth, sharp and gleaming, seemed unbelievably large to the small boy whose face had been pushed up against the fence.

Jack yelled, "You wanna steal from me? I'm gonna feed you to my dogs! Luis, grab the dogs and bring them here."

Sampson could smell the breath of the excited dogs as they ran around furiously, snarling, growling, and barking at the two boys, who trembled on the other side of the fence. The dogs were then removed from their cage and were now face-to-face with the terrified boys. The only force holding the animals back was Luis, who held the dogs lightly with a thin leather leash. Standing on their hind legs, the dogs were pulling Luis forward, trying to get a taste of Sampson and Noody.

After what seemed like an eternity, Jack finally released Sampson and Noody from his grip and moved them away from the dogs' cage.

Sampson, breathing hard, but refusing to cry, blurted out, "I'm sorry."

Jack ignored him. "Get out of my store and never come back!"

Sampson and Noody took off like terrified little rabbits. *Never again*, Sampson thought as he ran home in terror. *I swear. Never again.*

But never is a very long time.

TEMPTATION AND ITS CONSEQUENCES

As children, it was easy to think we could be successful thieves. We saw robbers and bad guys on television, and it wasn't difficult to put ourselves in those roles, especially if, from our point of view, we felt the need was great. Actually, we probably never even thought of it as stealing. We were just thirsty kids on a hot day who needed a quick and easy cooldown. In those days we didn't have any money and had to find ways to get by. It's always easy to make up a reason in your own mind to justify doing something that is just plain wrong. Perhaps because we were constantly exposed to crime and negative people like the Bomb, we unconsciously copied the behavior that surrounded us.

We never thought about the consequences and never even considered that our stealing could get us in deep trouble. Jack's homemade theft-prevention program of terrifying little thieves like us with his dogs proved to be a life-changing event for me. Today I can look back and laugh, but on that day I truly thought the two German shepherds would eat us alive. Snarling and drooling, with death in their eyes, they may have saved us from a potential life of crime. ■

CHAPTER FIVE

"HOW MUCH DO YOU NEED?"

RAMECK, AGE 12 Rameck, a sturdy, tough seventh-grader at Hubbard Middle School in Plainfield, New Jersey, headed home from the gifted and talented program that met after school once a week. He rode in his grandmother's red Chevy Caprice Classic, a long and comfortable car that perfectly fit her style. He loved it when she could pick him up. It was only in this car he could talk to Ma and work out some of the frustrations and confusion he felt.

"You like being in this program, Rameck?" his grandmother asked.

"Yeah, Mrs. Hatt looks me right in my face and tells me I'm intelligent. Not just smart—intelligent. I like that word," he said proudly. "She makes me feel like I can maybe be somebody."

"I tell you that all the time, boy," Ma said as she smoothly turned the corner.

"I know, but you're 'sposed to tell me stuff like that. Mrs. Hatt is different."

"Has she been there the whole time you been in this program?" his grandmother asked.

"Yeah, except for third and fourth grade, when I couldn't go because I was in Catholic school. And you *know* how that went!"

Ma laughed. "That was a real disaster. It's a good thing your mama ran out of money about the same time she ran out of patience with those nuns. Imagine, putting my grandson in special ed!"

"Hey, Ma, I need some new shoes," Rameck said, changing the subject.

"What's wrong with the ones you got on?"

"They're old and beat-up. The kids at school got these cool new sneakers made by Nike. I want some shoes with a swoosh." He knew it sounded stupid to her.

Ma laughed. "You must be a fool, boy. You want shoes with a swoosh, whatever that is, and your mama can't pay the rent? How much these shoes cost?"

"They only cost fifty dollars." Even as he said it, Rameck could predict how she would respond. She liked to quote well-worn proverbs and wise sayings whenever she had the chance to teach one of her many children or grandchildren.

"Boy, you don't have a pot to pee in, nor a window to throw it out. Don't try to live high off the hog. The shoes you're wearing will do just fine until next school year, when you've out-

"I BELIEVE IN YOU, RAMECK. I WANT YOU TO HAVE THE BEST."

grown them." To close the matter, she changed the subject. "Didn't you tell me you were going to try out for another play at school?"

Rameck sighed and looked out the window. He gave up on the shoes. Talking about being in plays, however, always cheered him up. "Yeah, I did. I got the part."

"What's the name of the play?" his grandmother asked.

"*The Wiz.* I got a big part."

"Well, I'm mighty proud of you!"

Rameck grinned. "The teacher, Miss Scott, said I had real good acting ability. Maybe I'll move away from here and be a movie star and make a million dollars. Then I can buy *you* some shoes with a swoosh, too!"

They both laughed. "As much as you sing and dance around here, boy, you're a natural for the movies," his grandmother commented.

"I really like being in plays," Rameck told her dreamily.

"How come?" she asked.

"Well, for one thing, there are always lots of girls around and lots of free time backstage." He looked at his grandmother out of the corner of his eye.

"A ladies' man—just like your daddy," his grandmother teased.

"But the real reason," Rameck told her honestly, "is the applause. I love it when the curtains go up, when I hear the people in the room laugh or react to what we're doing onstage.

But mostly, I love it when the show is over, and everybody claps and applauds and cheers. It's like they're all telling me I'm cool, I'm wonderful, I'm the best thing in the world."

"I understand," she said softly.

"Hey, Ma," Rameck began, "Miss Scott is starting a drama class, and I have a chance to maybe get real acting jobs." He hesitated. "I know you said I couldn't get the shoes, but this is different. I need some photographs—a portfolio—so Miss Scott can send them out to producers and stuff."

"How much do you need?"

"A hundred and fifty dollars," Rameck admitted. He waited while she sucked in her breath and exhaled noisily.

"Goodness, child!" she exclaimed.

"I figured if you said yes to the shoes, I would say I didn't really want them if you could help me get the pictures instead."

"That's an awful lot of money. You trying to play me, boy?" She didn't sound angry.

"No, ma'am." Rameck replied honestly. "The last day to pay the fee for the pictures is tomorrow," he added.

"Why you wait until the last minute to ask?"

Rameck lowered his head. "I knew it was more money than we got."

The Caprice rolled to a stop in front of the apartment where Rameck lived with his mother and new baby sister.

"I got my house payment here in my purse," Ma said slowly. "You know how proud I am to own that house, boy. But I suppose I can borrow from my cousins and stall the mortgage man a couple of days."

Rameck looked at her with hope. "Would you do that for me?" he asked.

"I might."

"I'd do anything you ask me—forever!" Rameck said, pleading.

"You'll do that anyway," Ma replied with a chuckle. "You understand what a sacrifice this is?"

"Oh, yes, ma'am."

"I don't know—sounds to me like it's for some foolishness."

"If I get these pictures, I can get parts in real movies, in shows in New York. I think I got talent, Ma."

"So does every other out-of-work actor in the world," she replied while looking at Rameck with a grim smile.

"I promise to make you proud of me," Rameck said.

Ma sighed again. "I know, boy. You come by my house in the morning, and I'll give it to you. I believe in you, Rameck. I want you to have the best."

"Can't you give it to me now? I have to be at school real early tomorrow," Rameck asked.

"I love your mama, but I don't trust her," his grandmother explained. "She's got demons that eat at her soul."

"I *promise*," Rameck pleaded. "She won't even know I have it."

His grandmother looked doubtful, but she reached into her large pocketbook and pulled out a wad of money. "This is for your future, you hear?" She handed it to Rameck, who hugged her tightly.

"Yes, ma'am," Rameck replied with excitement. "I love you, Ma. Thank you so much. I promise to make you proud of me."

"I'm already proud of you, boy. Your mama is, too, whether you know it or not. Don't screw this up."

"Yes, ma'am," Rameck promised again. The red Chevy Caprice roared away.

When Rameck walked into his house, the first thing he noticed was the silence. The television and radio, which ran constantly whether anyone paid any attention to them or not, were quiet. His baby sister, Mecca, lay asleep in her crib.

His mother, smoking a cigarette, sat at the kitchen table. "They turned off the electricity," she said in greeting.

"I see," Rameck replied. "We've been through this before. It won't be so bad. It's not very cold outside this time."

"I spent up my paycheck, and I got a refrigerator full of groceries that'll spoil," she told him bleakly.

Rameck thought back to the good times, when his mother had a well-paying job that she enjoyed, when she laughed all the time, when she took him to Disney World. Somehow, things had changed since his little sister had been born. "When can you pay the bill?" Rameck asked, thinking guiltily of the money in his pocket.

"Today is Thursday. I doubt if I can get the money together until Monday. That's a whole weekend with no electricity." She sighed, her eyes glazed and dull as she looked at her son. "What am I gonna do?" she asked plaintively.

"I don't know," Rameck said uncomfortably. He knew his little sister needed milk. He couldn't let her go hungry while he pursued some impossible Hollywood dream. He shifted from one foot to the other.

"You got any money?" his mother asked.

"No," he lied. "Where would I get that kind of money?" He wanted those pictures so badly, but guilt ripped at him. Mecca wasn't even two years old. She deserved cold milk and fresh food.

"You sure?" his mother asked. "You look to me like you holdin', boy."

Rameck sighed. He knew he would never have another chance to get that portfolio of photographs made. But he reached down into his pocket and slowly pulled out the hundred and fifty dollars. Reluctantly he handed it to his mother.

"You're the best!" she said cheerfully. "Where'd you get this?" she then asked suspiciously. "You ain't selling no drugs, are you? 'Cause I'll kick your butt if I find out you're messing with drugs."

Rameck wanted to tell her that long ago he had sworn to himself that he would never, ever get involved with drugs because he had seen what drugs could do to people he knew and loved, what drugs were doing to her, but he just shook his head. "Ma gave it to me for some pictures at school," he told her quietly.

"I promise I'll pay you back, baby. Next week for sure."

Rameck walked away from her sadly. The next morning, the stove and refrigerator were not back on, but his mother had taken the food to a neighbor's house. Mecca's milk was cold; her food was fresh; and Rameck's money, as well as that opportunity, was gone.

DREAMS AND
MISSED OPPORTUNITIES

I might have been an actor. If I had, I might have been a famous movie star by now. Acting was something I really wanted to do. I enjoyed it more than anything else at that time. But sometimes we are forced to make difficult decisions.

I honestly believe I had what it took to make it in show business. That money was the ticket to all of my dreams, but I gave it up. Giving my mother that money was one of the hardest decisions I ever had to make. I chose not to be selfish and to do what I thought was best for the family.

My mother had a lot of struggles she was dealing with, specifically drug addiction. That addiction made a mess of my household and tore our family apart. I was already the product of a single-family household, but with drugs added to the mix, it made a recipe for disaster.

And even though she didn't use the money like she said she would, if I had to do it over, I would do the same thing. Only this time I would make sure she used the money to get the electricity turned back on. In life you are going to have to make some hard decisions. Always try and make sure you make them with the very best intentions. If you do that, no matter what you decide and no matter what the outcome, it will be the right decision, because you made it for the right reasons. ■

CHAPTER SIX

"ARE YOU GODZILLA OR KING KONG?"

GEORGE, AGE 11 By the time he was eleven, most of the kids in his class were taller than George. He wore his hair cut short, instead of in a big Afro like many of the other boys. He made good grades; had lots of friends; and walked with a lanky, confident gait. When he smiled, which was often, it was clear to everyone that the teeth in his mouth had grown a little like George had—cheerfully and with an independent spirit. They were seriously crooked.

"Your first dentist appointment is this afternoon," his mother reminded him. "I'll pick you up at noon."

"I get out of school early—cool!" George replied. "Do I have to go back to school after I'm finished at the dentist?"

"No, I suppose not, but make sure you get your makeup work before you leave," his mother warned sternly.

"No problem," George said, almost dancing because anything to get him out of school in the middle of the day was worth celebrating. George was still an excellent student, consistently making good grades, but free days were rare and to be treasured.

When they got to the dental clinic, George looked around with interest. Pictures and charts of teeth decorated the walls, along with pictures of smiling toothbrushes and toothpaste taking a bow. He'd been to the dentist before, for cleanings and such, but somehow this visit seemed different.

While he and his mother waited their turn, George stood up and looked closely at pictures of teeth from various angles, teeth with decay and cavities, and teeth with braces attached.

"Is this what my teeth will look like after I get my braces?" he asked his mother.

"I don't know, son. I suppose," his mother replied.

"Does it hurt?"

"Again, I really don't know," she told him. "I've never had braces."

"How will I eat corn on the cob?"

His mother laughed. "Probably you just won't!"

George heard his name being called then, and he walked back to the examining room. A technician sat him in the dental chair, which was surprisingly comfortable; placed a paper bib on his chest; and attached it with a little metal chain.

"First we do X-rays," the technician explained, "so we can see your teeth and gums all the way down to the root system."

"I got ya," George replied with a nod.

"After that's done, the dentist will come in and examine your mouth."

"Will I get my braces today?"

"Not quite yet," the technician replied with a laugh. "Don't rush it. Most likely you'll be wearing braces for several years."

George thought about that and wondered if braces would interfere with his talking to girls. *Naw,* he said to himself. *I'm so cool, braces won't even matter!*

After the X-rays, the dentist walked into the room with an air of casual confidence. He wore a white coat and carried a clipboard in his hand. "I'm Dr. Thomas," he said, shaking George's hand firmly. "Are you ready for this adventure?"

George, not the least bit frightened or concerned, said, "Let's do it!"

The dentist took his time and showed George the X-rays, pointing out where his teeth were crowded and which teeth might need to be removed.

"You're gonna pull some of my teeth?"

"Probably just these two," the dentist replied. "You won't miss them, and your other teeth will thank me, because they'll have room to breathe."

"Will they grow back?" George asked.

"No, these are your permanent teeth," the dentist told him patiently.

"Does it hurt when the braces get put on?"

"Not much. I have magic fingers that are very gentle. Promise."

"Will my teeth look good when this is finished?" George touched his crooked teeth with his tongue.

"Your smile will be so fine that girls will fall at your feet. Guaranteed."

George laughed. "How do you hook the braces on?" he wanted to know next.

"Very carefully!" the dentist said with a laugh.

Dr. Thomas showed George every single step of the process, named all the instruments, and even let him take home some of the gummy material he used to make impressions of the inside of George's mouth.

"This is a nice job, man," George observed. "You make a lot of cash?"

"I do all right," the dentist replied with a smile.

"Let me ask you something else," George said, frowning with a bit of confusion. He thought for a moment, then asked, "Which is better, dentists or doctors? I mean, are doctors ranked higher than you? What I mean is, like if Godzilla fought King Kong, Godzilla would win. Are you Godzilla or King Kong?"

"I follow you," the dentist said, laughing. "Let me explain. A dentist *is* a doctor. After college, doctors go to medical school. Dentists go to dental school. Same amount of time and effort and study. But me, I'm like Superman—I'd beat both Godzilla *and* King Kong!" George laughed at Dr. Thomas, who was flexing his arms like he was ready to beat up a monster.

IT WAS LIKE DR. THOMAS HAD PLUGGED IN A CORD THAT BUZZED WITH ELECTRICITY AND EXCITEMENT.

George couldn't figure out why all this seemed so fascinating to him today. But it was like Dr. Thomas had plugged in a cord that buzzed with electricity and excitement. "When do I come back?" George asked.

"Two weeks," Dr. Thomas replied. "We'll do the first fitting of your braces then. It's going to be a long, slow process."

"Will you be my dentist every time I come back?" George asked.

"Absolutely," Dr. Thomas replied. "For as long as I'm assigned to this area. I'm a resident, which means we'll have a couple of years together. You'll have to come back every month at first and later every few months."

"Will I get out of school every time I come here?"

"I'll make sure of it," Dr. Thomas replied with a laugh.

"Sweet!" George replied. He couldn't wait until the next time.

THE BEGINNINGS OF A DREAM

Who would have thought that an ordinary trip to the dentist could turn into an extraordinary, life-changing event? I walked into that dentist's office unaware of the fact that he held the keys to my future in his interest in me. Something clicked when I looked at those dental charts, X-rays, and instruments. The dentist sensed my fascination and took the time to teach me and encourage me. He was eager to feed my inquisitive mind, and I was a willing sponge, soaking up all the information and inspiration he could give me.

Even though I had no idea how the dream of becoming a dentist could ever come true, I knew the moment I walked into that office that I had found what I wanted to do for the rest of my life. It took almost fourteen years of hard work and sacrifice from the day it first started to its accomplishment, but nothing is sweeter than making a dream come true.

Sometimes the smallest, most insignificant events in life can develop into something large, important, and life-changing. Look for those moments and grab on to the possibilities. ■

CHAPTER SEVEN

"YEAH, MAN. THEY SAY THE DRIVER'S DEAD."

SAMPSON, AGE 11 "You scared to go over to the cemetery, man?" a boy named Crusher taunted Sampson.

"No, man. I ain't scared of no dead people. It's the live ones that can get you!" Sampson, Crusher, a skinny kid named Razor, and several other boys headed across the street to the graveyard, each one making sure the others saw no fear in him.

"I heard this Reggie dude is pretty cool," Sampson said to his brother Andre.

"Yeah," Andre replied. "Reggie's tight. He's the best kung fu teacher in New Jersey." Andre had taken lessons from Reggie for a couple of years, and Sampson wanted to see what all the talk was about.

"I heard Reggie was in a martial arts movie," Crusher volunteered.

"I'd sure rather live in Hollywood instead of Newark," Razor commented. "How'd he end up working as a security guard at a graveyard?"

"That's a pretty boring job," Sampson said with a laugh. "It's not like the folks he's watching are gonna get up and walk away!" The group of boys hurried through the cemetery and over to the main building, where memorial services were held. They paused at the huge mahogany doors.

"How long has he been doing this?" Sampson whispered to his brother.

"For a while now," Andre explained. "I told you—he's really cool. He says it's his way of giving back—whatever that means."

The doors swung open then, and Reggie—tall, broad-shouldered, and powerfully muscled, greeted them with a large smile. "Welcome, young brothers," he began. He lined up the boys, then showed them different kung fu moves and how to relax by closing their eyes and breathing deeply.

Sampson inhaled and listened carefully as Reggie spoke. "Calm your mind," he said quietly. "Forget about outside problems. Concentrate your thoughts on a positive flow of energy."

"You gonna teach us how to fight?" Razor asked.

"No," Reggie replied. "I'm going to teach you how to live."

Sampson and his friends loved to watch martial arts TV shows and movies. After watching one of those, they all practiced their jumps and kicks and fake karate attacks on each other. He thought maybe Reggie would teach them how to knock down ten people with one whirling jump and kick, like they did on TV.

"Any fool can fight," Reggie said calmly. "It takes a man to know when to use his mind instead of his body. Repeat after me," he continued. "Toughen my sinews, harden my bones, strengthen my mind."

Sampson repeated it with feeling. This Reggie dude seemed to have it all together. He was big and strong, and Sampson was sure that Reggie could win in any fistfight, but Reggie's strength seemed to come from someplace other than his fists.

Every Sunday Sampson and his friends went to the graveyard to listen to Reggie's Newark-style Chinese philosophy and to practice the ancient art of kung fu. They learned body stances like the Black Crane and the Praying Mantis, as well as body-strengthening techniques. Sampson loved it.

"Consider a single drop of water," Reggie said one day when it was pouring rain. "Alone, it is harmless, gentle, and powerless. But everyone respects the power of the sea. You are an ocean. Pull together each drop of your energy to find yourself. No one can destroy the ocean."

"FIND OTHERS WITH GOALS LIKE YOURS AND STICK WITH THEM."

After the lesson that afternoon, Sampson said to Reggie, "I know what you're saying, man, but sometimes I feel like I'm under the ocean, you know what I mean? Like I'm drowning and can't get out."

"Little Man, I like your questions—you're a deep thinker, and you ask like a man. The only way to save yourself from the drugs and the temptation and the violence all around you is to find the strength within yourself," Reggie replied. Sampson liked the fact that Reggie had given him that nickname.

"What if I can't find any strength?" Sampson asked quietly.

Reggie told Sampson, "You have unbelievable intelligence and potential. Instead of letting stuff overpower and drown you, you have to use your brain to BE the ocean. Find others with goals like yours, and stick with them. You see what I'm saying, Little Man?"

Sampson nodded and sighed, but he really had no idea how to fit all this cool-sounding kung fu philosophy with dealers who offered him two hundred dollars just to run some drugs across town. Getting in trouble was so much easier than pretending to be an ocean.

Two days later, even though he hadn't even meant to do anything wrong, Sampson was arrested for shoplifting. It wasn't even his fault.

"Yo, Sampson, you want to go into business with me, man?" seventeen-year-old Eddie asked Sampson.

"What kind of business?" Sampson asked warily. He had known Eddie ever since grammar school and knew that Eddie had been in trouble with the police several times, so he wanted to feel out the situation before giving an answer.

"It's all legal, man. I'm straight. I'm gonna start me a carpet-cleaning company."

"That sounds good," Sampson replied. "I always wanted to

be a professional. Things are pretty tough at home, and I could use a gig."

"I need workers—men to help me clean up places like office buildings and stuff. I'll pay you good money."

"How much?" Sampson asked.

"I don't know yet, but it will be good," Eddie replied.

Sampson, always looking for creative ways to make some dollars, thought this would be a good opportunity. It sounded more lucrative than helping people at the local grocery store bag their groceries or carry the bags to their cars for loose change. Any legitimate way that he could earn a little extra money sounded okay to Sampson. "When do I start?" Sampson asked.

"Well, your first job is to help me get the equipment. It's waiting for me at the store."

Sampson figured his mother and even Reggie would be proud of him for making a wise judgment call. After all, Sampson had always considered himself a sharp decision maker. The two boys walked a mile to the store, then wandered around inside for a few minutes, looking at the equipment.

As they were leaving, Eddie, whose hands were full, said to Sampson, "Grab that machine for me, man. We're ready to go."

Sampson walked over to the heavy carpet-cleaning machine and slowly pushed it out the front door of the store. It was too heavy to carry, so he pushed it carefully down the sidewalk, in full view of people walking and cars driving.

Halfway down the block Sampson heard a police siren as a patrol car stopped right next to him. He looked around in genuine surprise as the police officers jumped out of their car and grabbed him. "Where did you get that machine, boy?" one of the cops asked him.

"From the store back there," Sampson answered honestly. "It's for my friend Eddie's new cleaning business."

"And who is this Eddie?" the officer asked.

Sampson looked down the street. He could just barely see the back of Eddie, running away as fast as he could, about to disappear around a corner.

Sampson's heart thudded in his chest. *How could Eddie play me?* he thought. Instead of understanding what had happened, the police officer only saw a boy on the sidewalk with a stolen machine. Sampson felt his hands being pulled behind him and the handcuffs being laced to his wrists. He was in total disbelief.

The police tossed him in their car, took him to headquarters, and booked him for shoplifting. No matter how he tried to explain his innocence, no one wanted to listen. Being set up was the same as being guilty, it seemed, and no one had much sympathy for him.

Sitting in a small cell that smelled vaguely of disinfectant, Sampson fumed and planned how he was going to get revenge on Eddie. He knew he would eventually have to call his mother. The police planned to transfer him to the juvenile home the next morning.

A police officer approached the cell. "Your brother is here to get you," he told Sampson as he unlocked the door. Sampson looked up in surprise. He wondered how his brother knew that he was in jail.

When he got to the front desk, Sampson saw not his brother, but Eddie's older brother, Ronald, standing there, pretending to be Sampson's family member. Ronald told the police the same story Sampson told them earlier. Sampson said nothing, afraid the police would figure out who Ronald really was. Finally, they allowed Ronald to sign Sampson out. The police eventually believed Sampson, and the charges were dropped.

When Sampson and Ronald got outside, Eddie was hiding on the other side of the precinct building. Sampson ran over to Eddie and, with a curse, immediately punched him square in his face. The two boys starting fighting, falling to the ground, taking turns exchanging licks. Sampson had never been so angry.

Ronald broke them up. "Quit it before the police come out here!" The boys knew the wisdom of his advice, so they brushed themselves off and walked toward home.

Eddie turned to Sampson. "I'm sorry, man. I didn't mean to put you out there. I thought we could get away with it and start a business."

Sampson, still angry, muttered, "You didn't have to play me like that." He kicked at a rock in the dirt.

Eddie continued, "If I truly meant to play you, I never would have gotten my brother to take a chance coming up here to the station. You know he's got a warrant for his arrest in the next town."

Sampson retorted, "Yeah, but it was you that got me in this mess."

"Yeah, I know," said Eddie, his head hanging low.

"Just forget it, man," Sampson said finally. "It's over." He threw his arm around Eddie's shoulder. "At least my moms didn't find out."

The next day, all of the projects were buzzing with the news that Sampson had been locked up. Many of his friends thought it was cool that he had finally been arrested.

"Yo, Sampson, you finally earned your stripes, dog."

"Now you know what it's like being a prisoner of the Man," another said.

Sampson joked with them and acted like the whole experience was exciting. "Man, those police didn't have nothing on me. I sat back in that room, smiling, tellin' them to call my lawyer!" He never let on how mad he was at Eddie, although he had already decided to forgive him. After all, he had known Eddie all of his life.

Two weeks later, the sound of metal crunching against itself, piercing sirens, and an angry explosion jarred Sampson awake. Confused by the noise and commotion outside, Sampson stumbled out of bed and peeked out of his bedroom window. It was six A.M., and still dark outside, but the predawn shadows were illuminated by flashing police car lights and the fire that burned from the engine of the 1984 Pontiac that was wrapped around the telephone pole just a few feet from Sampson's door.

Police sirens, car chases, and even gunshots were common sounds around Ludlow Street and in the projects. These noises decorated the night just as the chirping of birds and crickets was commonplace in the country. But this event was right by Sampson's house, and everyone in the neighborhood was stumbling outside to check out the excitement.

Sampson grabbed a jacket, stuffed his feet into some sneakers, and hurried out to see the accident up close. The morning air was chilly and smelled faintly of last night's rain. Sampson shivered as he watched firefighters spray the blaze and paramedics attempt to remove the driver from what used to be a car. Police officers seemed to be everywhere.

"Anybody know who it is?" Sampson heard a neighbor ask.

"Never seen that car 'round here. Must be stolen," someone replied.

"Police was chasin' him, and he flew 'round that corner with them right on his tail," another neighbor reported. "I saw the whole thing."

"Anybody get hurt?" Sampson asked.

"Yeah, man. They say the driver's dead."

Just then Sampson saw them pull the bloody body of the driver from the car. "That's Lucille's boy!" someone screamed. "Oh, my Lord, her boy is dead! Go 'round the corner and tell his mama to get out here quick."

But Sampson just stood there in stunned disbelief. The driver of the car was Razor Sizemore. His real name was Raymond, but everybody called him Razor because he was so skinny. Razor, who had stopped coming to Reggie's kung fu classes because he had become a runner for the drug dealers; Razor, with the sad smile and the desperation in his eyes; Razor, who had sat right next to Sampson in Miss Bellingham's math class just two days before. Razor, who died that crispy, cool morning while running from police in a car that he had stolen, had just turned twelve years old.

LIVING AND DYING ON THE STREETS

I couldn't believe it when Razor died. Even though by age eleven I had seen more than my share of death and dying, Razor was a kid just like me. Actually, his death could easily have been mine. Given the opportunity at that age, I might have been foolish enough to try to steal a car—just for the thrill of the chase. But the streets could easily take a kid's life—whether by drugs or guns or fights or just plain reckless behavior. So much precious untapped talent is lost to the ills of the streets.

As for Eddie, we remained tight for several years, but our lives drifted in different directions. As fast as I saw my life progress in a positive direction, Eddie's life fell apart even faster. He became a victim to the drug scene, perhaps because he realized that the streets offered him no love, or perhaps because he could no longer take the frustration of being on the bottom of society with no means of escape. I'm ever thankful that my life turned out differently.

People like Reggie, who volunteered his time and knowledge to the kids of the community, who knew the value of giving back, proved to be an important influence on my life at that time. I found myself constantly reaching out to anyone who offered a positive position. I was thirsty for someone to let me know I could be a success. ■

CHAPTER EIGHT

"I DON'T EVEN KNOW ANYBODY WHO WENT TO COLLEGE."

SAMPSON AND GEORGE, AGE 12 "Yo, Sampson, what did you get on your report card?" a boy named Tito asked him one day after school. Grades had been given out for the end of sixth grade, and Sampson had made the honor roll once more. In spite of the fact he played around in school and sometimes gave the teacher a hard time, Sampson rarely got any grade lower than a B.

"Aw, man, you know how it is," Sampson responded vaguely.

"That teacher be cheatin' us, man. Did she flunk you in math and science, like she did me?"

"Yeah, she be trippin'." Sampson hoped Tito would never see his report card, on which he had received an A in both science and math. When other kids in his class happened to see a good grade on a test paper that was handed back to Sampson, he would tell them he had cheated on the test instead of admitting he had studied.

When Sampson got home, however, he told his mother proudly, "I got the honor roll again, Moms. Me and my boys are gonna rule Dayton Street Elementary next year."

"I don't want you running with those hoodlums," she replied.

"They're not hoodlums—they're my boys," he tried to explain. "I been waiting ever since first grade to get to seventh grade and take over the school!" Dayton Street Elementary School went up to grade eight. The older students always demanded respect from the younger kids. Sampson could not wait for his turn.

"You're not going there next year," his mother announced.

"What do you mean?" Sampson asked angrily.

"Your teacher called me. She said you're already reading at a ninth-grade level. Do you know what that means to me, Sampson?" she asked quietly.

Sampson looked up at the ceiling and replied, "Yeah, Moms. I know." Sampson's mother had been forced to drop out of school at an early age because of the death of her mother and had never learned to read. So Sampson knew how important his accomplishments were for her.

"Your grades are high, your future is bright, and you should go to University High School."

"That's way on the other side of town!" Sampson protested. "I'd have to take two buses every day just to get there!"

"That school can give you a better education, boy. You could even go to college!"

"What do I care about college?" he yelled. "I don't even know anybody who went to college."

"All your teachers have college degrees," she reasoned.

"They don't count." Sampson slumped in a chair.

"University High School is your key, son. I'm not going to let you miss this chance."

"But I really don't want to go there!" Sampson exclaimed once more, even though he knew he had lost this battle. He thought of one last quick escape from his new future. Surely this one would work. "Instead of being the top kid in the school, I'd be at the bottom!"

"Tough cookies," his mother said. "The test is Saturday."

Sampson stomped off, but he knew better than to keep arguing with his mother. On Saturday, he grimly boarded the first bus to take him to University High School, and he was pleased to see a friend of his from school.

"You taking the test for University, Craig?" Sampson asked hopefully.

"Yeah, man. My mom is making me." The two boys rode in silence, each glad the other was along for company.

When they arrived at the school, dozens of kids were taken to a room where the test was administered. The school was large, much bigger than Dayton Street Elementary, and kids from all over Newark had been asked to take the test.

Sampson looked over the group, figured he was at least as smart as everyone else, and sat down at a desk near the back of the room. Craig took a seat next to him. On the other side of Sampson sat a tall, lanky kid with braces on his teeth.

"What's up, man," the boy said.

"Chillin'," Sampson replied with a careless shrug.

They said nothing else to each other. Sampson noticed, however, that the boy seemed to speed through the questions as if they were really easy. He figured if this kid could do that, he could, too. Sampson wasn't crazy about leaving Dayton Street Elementary, but he couldn't stand the idea that there might be kids learning things he wouldn't be taught. He hated to think that somebody at another school might know more than he did. He hated to be beaten at anything. So he did his best on the test.

He and the kid with the braces finished at the same time.

ENTERING SEVENTH GRADE

Although I can recall almost nothing about that test, it was another turning point in my life. Being chosen to take the test was an honor, a recognition of being one of the best students in the city. Passing the test and being accepted into University High School opened a door for me that led to the possibility of achieving my dreams, which were still being formed and clarified in my mind.

I don't really remember that Sam and I sat together, although we certainly could have. Dozens of kids from around the city were assembled in that room on that day. Neither Sam nor I could know that our lives had just intersected, and we would eventually become the best of friends. We were just two seventh-graders who were taking advantage of an opportunity. Rameck, by the way, did not come to University High School until ninth grade. That's when Sam and I met him, and the three of us eventually formed a friendship that would last a lifetime.

University High School included grades seven through twelve, so when school started in the fall, it was much more impressive and massive than anything either Sam or I had experienced in grade school. For the first time in my life, I had different teachers for different subjects. The class that stood out for me that first year was science, taught by Mr. Moore. He had a way of making science stimulating as well as challenging. Again, I did not know it at the time, but he was preparing me for my future. ▪

MAKING GOOD GRADES

When I was in school, a good grade could destroy a kid. High marks could open you up to ridicule, to name-calling, to being made an outsider. I never understood the mentality that made failing equal to being cool. As far as I was concerned, kids who failed in school were losers. They couldn't get jobs, had no chance of going to college, had no hope for their future. I thought failing was pretty dumb. I still do.

For me, school was always easy and didn't take much effort, but I know that many people struggle to do well and maintain high goals. I respect anyone who does his or her best to reach his greatest potential. I was able to navigate the unspoken rules of the culture of a school community. I managed to be one of the "cool" kids while excelling in school at the same time. Lots of kids actually admired me for my good grades and academic achievements.

If others make fun of you because you do well in school, don't let that be a deterrent. It's stupid to fail, especially if you do it on purpose. It's smart to grab what you can from the teachers and lessons around you. Life is rough—you need all the knowledge you can get to succeed. Be proud of your academic success. ■

CHAPTER NINE

"YOU KIDS ARE GONNA GET YOURSELF KILLED."

RAMECK, NINTH GRADE "What's today, my fine fellow?" said Rameck onstage, dressed as Scrooge in the Charles Dickens play, *A Christmas Carol*. His hair and face had been powdered to make him look old, and he peered out of a stage window at another student who was dressed as a little boy.

"Today?" replied the boy. "Why, it's Christmas Day!"

Rameck beamed, told the boy in his best old-man stage voice to go and buy a turkey and deliver it, then danced around on the stage because he had been allowed to live after his visit with the spirits of Christmas Past, Present, and Future. Rameck could feel the pleasure in the audience as mean old Scrooge was once again transformed. He knew he had the crowd under his spell.

The play rolled to its conclusion, and Rameck shouted in a booming voice, "As Tiny Tim has said many times, 'God bless us, every one!'"

Everyone watching exploded in applause, and the curtain came down. It rose again quickly, and the members of the cast came forward for their curtain calls. For each character—Tiny Tim, the ghosts, and others in the play—the audience, made up mostly of University High students and their parents, applauded enthusiastically. Rameck, as the star of the show, came out last. The rest of the cast parted for him to come to the front of the stage and take his bows. He walked regally and with great dignity, bowed low to the audience, breathing deeply in the glory of the spotlight, the cheers, and the thunderous applause just for him. *It doesn't get any better than this,* Rameck said to himself.

Although most students began the advanced academic program in the seventh grade, Rameck had transferred to University High School in the ninth grade. Usually students had difficulty adjusting to the rigorous classes, especially if they had not attended University the first two years, but Rameck slid in easily and made good grades from the beginning. He even had time to audition for the school play. In a huge upset, because a certain student who had been at the school for years always got the lead, Rameck beat him out for the part with ease.

"Good job, man," a ninth-grader with braces named George said to him after the show.

"Yeah, man. Really tight," his friend Sampson said.

Rameck nodded, took the praise, and moved on. He had

several classes with George and Sampson, but they were just two more dudes in the hall. He purposely hadn't made many friends at this new school yet. Rameck hadn't wanted to leave his friends and his old neighborhood to come to this school, but he liked the advanced math and science programs it offered, and he breezed through his classes with ease. So every day, as soon as school was out, he headed back to his old neighborhood to hang with "his boys." Sometimes he would even skip classes at University to run with the boys from Plainfield.

A couple of weeks later, Rameck found himself hanging out on the corner near Plainfield Elementary with his old friends, about ten of them.

"Glad you made it, man," a kid named Bookie said.

"Yeah, Rameck always come through for us," a skinny boy named Marley added with appreciation.

"What we gonna do today?" Bookie asked.

Shawn, who had done time in juvenile detention, as had Marley, said with bravado, "We goin' down to Arlington Avenue and whip somebody's butt!"

Nobody asked why. It might have had something to do with a comment one of the Arlington boys had made earlier—it didn't really matter. They didn't need much reason to fight. Rameck and the others put their hands in their pockets and sauntered down the sidewalks of Plainfield, looking for trouble, looking for somebody to beat up.

When they got to the bus stop, several of the Arlington Street boys yelled at them from cars driven by older kids, perhaps their older brothers. Rameck and his boys shouted back.

Finally Rameck said, "You think you so bad, why don't you get outta them cars and do something!"

The Arlington Street kids, about ten of them, jumped out of their cars and proceeded to punch and roll with Rameck and the Plainfield boys. Everybody squared off with one person, and the brawl began. One kid, a big guy with missing teeth, threw a punch at Rameck, who ducked, then darted back up, swung hard, and popped the kid in his face. The boy fell to the ground, another tooth dangling from his already broken mouth. He jumped up then, anger and fire in his eyes, and began to chase Rameck and his friends.

Just then, the city bus lumbered up to the stop, and the door opened. Rameck and his friends, anxious to get away in a hurry, jumped on the bus. It pulled away in a hiss of exhaust fumes.

"Whew! That was close," Rameck said, rubbing his fist. Punching that kid in the mouth had cut and bruised the back of his hand.

"It ain't over yet," Marley said. "They're gettin' in their cars and chasin' the bus!"

Rameck peered out of the bus window. Sure enough, the Arlington boys, looking angry enough to kill, were speeding behind the bus, which was pulling up to its next stop.

IT MIGHT HAVE HAD SOMETHING TO DO WITH A COMMENT ONE OF THE BOYS HAD MADE—IT DIDN'T REALLY MATTER. THEY DIDN'T NEED MUCH REASON TO FIGHT.

Bookie ran to the front of the bus and begged the bus driver, "Man, you can't let them kids on the bus! They gonna kill us!"

The bus driver, angry that these kids he considered to be hoodlums were using his bus as a part of their fight, retorted, "I'm not allowed to refuse anyone a ride on this bus. You kids take your fights and your foolishness elsewhere! You're endangering hard-working folks who just want to get home from work!"

The bus lumbered to a stop. The door opened. The kid that Rameck had punched in the mouth was the first to board. He waved a fifty-dollar bill. "This is for me and my fifteen buddies!" he said defiantly to the bus driver.

The driver looked at what was becoming a dangerous situation and said, "I don't have change for a fifty, son."

The boy just said, "Keep the change. I don't want to ride your bus anyway. I want these punks you got riding on it!" He grabbed Marley and tried to pull him off the bus, but Marley held on as tight as he could to the bus pole. Rameck and Bookie and the others pulled Marley's legs and got him back. The Arlington boy jumped off the bus then, and the bus sped off.

Rameck and the others sat quietly, trying to catch their breath and wondering what would happen when the bus reached the end of the line. The Arlington boys continued to follow the bus in their cars, patiently waiting for revenge.

By the time it reached the end of the line, no one was left on the bus except for Rameck and his friends. The Arlington boys were still right behind them. "If we can make it to my friend Drea's house, we'll be safe. He lives two blocks from here," Rameck suggested.

"We better be doin' some flyin'!" Bookie said.

"You boys are on your own now," the bus driver said. "Don't you have anything better to do?" he asked. "You kids are gonna get yourself killed."

Rameck thanked the driver for trying to help, but he and his friends had no choice but to walk down the steps of the bus and hope they could make it to Drea's house in time. They left the bus, feet flying, and ran as fast as they could through yards, over fences, and behind trees as the Arlington gang chased them down the streets.

Just as they got to Drea's house, Rameck heard a loud series of sharp explosions. Gunfire! He and his friends rolled to the porch and huddled in a corner. The Arlington boys, screaming obscenities, sped away in their cars.

Sitting up slowly, Rameck could see clearly several bullet holes in the wood of the front porch.

He breathed deeply, immensely relieved that he would live another day. He wondered where his life was heading and how he could manage to escape what seemed to be an increasingly downward spiral. He had no answers.

THE CALL OF THE STREETS

People often say you can pick your friends, but you can't pick your family. I beg to differ, at least in the community where I grew up. There, it was very difficult to pick your friends as well. We forged bonds with those who lived around us. We had no other choice.

Unfortunately, there was a lot of negative peer pressure in my neighborhood, so much so that it became the norm to do the wrong thing instead of the right thing. It was what your peers expected of you. If you didn't conform, you might be labeled "not cool."

When I was a teenager, I often found myself getting involved in dangerous and foolish activities, just so I'd fit in with those around me. I did a lot of things my gut told me I shouldn't do, things I really didn't want to do.

That's why I think it's important to talk about these issues. Getting good grades and staying out of trouble are really cool and really, really smart. It also makes you a leader, and that's cool, too. Take it from me; I know. Why? Because I was a follower. Most of my friends were as well.

It wasn't until I met Sam and George that I knew what positive peer pressure was all about. It took me some time to get it together, but when I did, it was the most wonderful feeling ever. For the first time, I truly felt like a leader. ■

CHAPTER TEN

"WHAT'S UP WITH THAT? YOU THINK YOU BETTER THAN US?"

SAMPSON, TENTH GRADE Sampson, George, and Rameck seemed to fall into each other's lives around the middle of the ninth grade. Rameck had watched and admired George and Sam's friendship from a distance at first, but soon, through sports as well as academics, the three of them ended up hanging together on a regular basis.

By tenth grade, they had forged a steady friendship. The classes were easy for the three of them, and they all enjoyed outsmarting the teachers and running the halls, taking every school rule to its limit. They found they had much in common—telling jokes, talking trash, laughing at crazy things their teachers did, shooting hoops in the gym, and listening to rap music as loud as they could crank it up.

IT WASN'T LIKE HE WANTED TO GET INTO TROUBLE—IT WAS JUST SO EASY TO DO SO.

Sampson, for one, was glad to have someone to share his thoughts with. Late one night the three of them sat in the empty bleachers at school. The night was clear, the moon was bright, and talk came easy.

"You think there's life on other planets?" George asked.

Rameck laughed. "Well, if there is, I hope they got it together better than we do down here."

"Too much drugs and crime down here," Sampson said.

"And killing," George added.

"And girls who won't go out with us," Rameck added with a chuckle.

"Speak for yourself, man." Sampson laughed. "I got more girls than I know what to do with! And I don't even have a car. Just me riding on my Nikes!"

"Why do you think kids at school think making good grades is stupid?" George asked.

"It's a school where everybody is supposed to be smart and do good. I don't get it," Rameck said.

"None of us really has a blueprint on how to make it," Sampson said. "Right now, all I know is I can't let the streets swallow me. I have to get mine."

"And what will that be?" Rameck asked him.

"I don't know yet. But I want more than what I see every day on the blocks," Sampson replied.

"You got that right," Rameck said.

"You ever have trouble telling your boys that you don't want to do something?" George asked quietly.

"All the time," the others answered together.

"I ain't scared of them," Rameck said, "and I ain't scared of what they think of me, but . . ."

". . . you don't want to look stupid or scared or weak," George finished for him.

"Yeah, something like that," Rameck agreed.

"A lotta times, it's just easier to go along than to say something," George added.

"But I ain't backing down from nobody!" Sampson asserted loudly. "They push me too far, and I'll give them something to think about!"

Rameck, who could also fight as easily as he could do a math problem in his head, nodded with understanding. "It's all about power, man."

"Sometimes it just feels good. You know, that rush you get when you're connecting with somebody's gut or when you're getting away with something wrong. You feel me?" Sampson asked.

"Yeah, man, I know what you're talkin' about," Rameck replied.

The talk faded as the night air got chilly, and they headed to their homes.

Sampson remembered that conversation well a few weeks later, when he walked with a friend named Frank down Ludlow Street one rainy night. They passed by what used to be Twin City Skating Rink, once known as the hottest rink in Newark. People had traveled from all parts of Newark to be a part of the skating crowd. It was only one block away from Dayton Street Projects. "Too bad they closed the skating rink," Sampson said with a sigh. "Good music, slick skates, plenty of fine girls hanging around, too."

"Yeah, man, but the police got tired of breaking up fights or taking reports from kids who got beat up or got their stuff stolen."

"If it wasn't for the bus, lots more kids would have been tromped by the Dayton Street boys," Sampson replied with a laugh. "You know, lots of them spent their days just waiting in front of the rink, spotting targets to attack and rip off."

"Well, you know Newark. You stay on your side of town, everything be fine. You come over here to the skating rink, you get your butt beat. That's just the way it is." Frank shrugged.

"After that murder last year, there was no way they'd keep the skating rink open," Sampson said. "Too bad," he repeated as the rain trickled down his back.

A man who looked vaguely familiar walked up to the two of them. "Hey, man, let me hold two dollars," he said to Frank.

"I don't got it," Frank replied.

"Man, I know you got two dollars. Don't play with me. Give me the money!"

"I don't got it," Frank repeated, loudly this time.

Without another word, the stranger, who was wearing a black goose-down jacket, lifted up his shirt and pulled out a gun.

Sampson tensed, ready for whatever he would have to do. "What about you?" the man asked. "I know you got two dollars."

Very calmly Sampson replied, "I ain't got it, man." Sampson

knew firsthand that many people in the neighborhood were desperate and wouldn't think twice about taking his life.

"What if I shoot both of you?" the man asked them angrily. "I could shoot you right now."

Sampson and Frank said nothing, but turned and walked away. Sampson waited for bullets to slice through his back. But he heard nothing but his thudding heart and the falling rain.

Sampson thought back to the days of his kung fu lessons with Reggie. It had all seemed so simple then. *Forget about outside problems*, Reggie had said. *Concentrate your thoughts on a positive flow of energy*. But Sampson knew he needed more than positive energy to escape angry men with guns. He felt trapped.

Several weeks later, January 19, to be exact, Sampson was celebrating his birthday with some friends. They decided the best way to do that was with a little beer and a little liquor. They drove around Newark, looking for a place to park and get right.

"Yo, man, it's your birthday," a dude named Hock said. "Light up and let's celebrate together." He gave Sampson a package of what appeared to be cocaine.

"Word up, word up," Sampson replied, not committing himself either way.

Hock suggested, "Let's make a 'woolly.'"

Sampson knew what a woolly was. He watched as Hock took the tobacco out of a regular cigarette and then mixed it with the cocaine. He then wrapped the loaded cigarette back into its paper. Hock lit it, then passed it to the guy sitting closest to him. The dude took two puffs, then zonked out. His head bounced against the back of the car seat.

Hock then offered it to Sampson. "It's your birthday, man. We love you, man. You go now."

Sampson hesitated. Even the smoke from the thing was making him feel dizzy. "Naw, man, that ain't me," he declared. Sampson wasn't tempted to do drugs the way many of his friends were. He'd seen too much destruction and devastation in their lives because of that. And he didn't like feeling out of control.

"What's up with that? You think you better than us?" Hock replied angrily.

"Naw, dog, I'm just too faded right now," Sampson said. "Besides, you know I don't get high."

They didn't like it, but they backed off, mostly because very soon all of them were too high to care. Sampson jumped out of the car and left them there, glad to be able to breathe fresh air and celebrate his birthday with a clear head and a clean conscience.

But it was hard for him. He knew his options were limited. He was reaching a point in life where the despair and negativity were threatening to take over his life.

A few months later, on a hot summer day, Sampson and a guy named Spud were kicking it on the corner. They were dressed like most of the boys in the neighborhood— jeans, sneakers, and white tank tops. The two of them had been friends ever since they were in Mrs. Davis' third-grade class together and had played on the same Pop Warner football team. Summer days were long, and summer programs didn't exist, so the two of them were left with lots of time and nothing to fill it with.

"Yo, man, I got a way for us to make some money," Spud said.

"What you got in mind?" asked Sampson.

"Put up some cash, we'll get some crack, then we'll split the profits. Easy money. Big money."

"Sounds good, man, but I don't know. I don't want to get caught up in no drug stuff," Sampson replied.

"It's not like drugs will dry up and die if you don't participate, man," Spud told him.

"Yeah, you got that right," Sampson said. He sure could use the money, and it would be nice to help his mother and family. Finances were tight around the house. His mother was always struggling to find ways to pay the mortgage, keep the electricity on, and feed all the children.

"Don't worry about it. Everybody's doin' it, man," Spud said. "Come with me tonight up to Harlem. I'll show you how it's done."

Sampson agreed, and late that night the two of them took a train all the way uptown to Harlem in New York City. They brought a girl with them so they wouldn't look too suspicious. They walked to an apartment where a man stood in the doorway wearing a gun in a holster. He patted them down, like Sampson had seen cops do on the street.

They entered a tiny room inside the house. It was filthy. Bags of drugs were piled on the tables. Men with large guns stood all around, ready to shoot in an instant. To Sampson, it looked like a scene from a movie. Spud and Sampson passed their money to the men, and in return they were given a plastic bag of crack cocaine. This was the first time that Sampson had ever picked up drugs.

As they stepped out of the house, Sampson looked up and noticed the misty rain glistening in the streetlight. *What have I gotten myself into?* he thought painfully.

"Easy score," Spud said, seemingly unaffected by the horror of the situation.

"Hey, man, I'm outta here," Sampson said suddenly. "You take all the money—all of it—this ain't me."

Instead of complaining, Spud just shrugged. "Catch you later, man." With that, he disappeared into the night. Sampson went home, relieved that once more he'd been able to navigate that delicate road between what was right and what was real.

SO EASY TO FALL INTO THE DRUG SCENE

I often imagined myself in a different world, one not filled with murder, drugs, gangs, crime, and negativity. But that was only my imagination, not my reality. Regardless of where I turned, there was always another malignant situation brewing, waiting for the right moment to take my life.

In spite of all that, I chose to turn away from the drug scene. I saw too many friends and family members succumb to its powerful destruction. When youth in my neighborhood looked for an outlet of expression, drugs were always easily available. Getting into the drug game was as easy as buying a ticket for the train or bus. But that was a trip I didn't want to take. If the way I managed to turn down drugs sounds like it wasn't extremely difficult, don't get me wrong—it was. Not only was it really hard, but it was continuous—every single day offered options to give up and give in. I saw many of my friends buy new cars, jewelry, and clothes with drug money they had earned. It would have been so easy to give in to the drug-induced, mind-numbing relief from the problems and despair all around me. I was driven and had to remain strong to avoid all the temptations.

I couldn't help but wonder why more wasn't being done to prevent the surplus of drug trafficking in urban neighborhoods like mine. It seemed to me like nobody really cared. The political powers were aware but never fully committed themselves to making a difference. ■

CHAPTER ELEVEN

"A STICKY WEB OF BRIGHT PINK SILLY STRING ACROSS THE ASTONISHED TEACHER'S FACE"

RAMECK, ELEVENTH GRADE "Yo, man, what's up with this? How come there's no black history classes taught at this school?" Rameck asked the history teacher as he flipped through the pages of their American history book. "All I see in here is white folks!"

"We teach the history of all Americans, Rameck," the teacher replied carefully. "We try very hard to be culturally diverse in our approach."

"Where?" Rameck asked bluntly. "I see a picture of some slaves, and three hundred pages later I see Martin Luther King. Didn't anybody black or Hispanic do anything important in all that time?"

The teacher changed the subject, saying it was time for class to begin, but Rameck seethed inside. He had recently helped organize a group at school called the United Students Organization, with Ahi and Amiri Baraka, sons of the famous poet Amiri Baraka, and another student named Hassan. The USO met regularly, not to cause trouble, but to try to work within the school and the community to make changes.

George and Sampson went to meetings occasionally, but Rameck, always questioning, was one of the leaders.

"Our history books should reflect our history," Ahi said.

"And we need more money in this school," Hassan added with passion. "Why do they always cut the budgets of schools in the city? Suburban kids have swimming pools and tennis courts and carpet in the halls. We get the leftover desks and old books and equipment. We deserve better!"

"We ought to walk out!" Rameck suggested at one meeting.

"And what would that do," George asked, "except get us in trouble?"

But Ahi seized upon the idea. "If just a few of us walk out, you're right, we would get in trouble. But suppose we ALL walk out—the entire school?" he asked excitedly.

Rameck grabbed his excitement. "Suppose we get other schools in Newark to walk with us? They would *have* to pay attention to us!"

"It would have to be well organized," Ahi said. "We need flyers and coordinators and troubleshooters. We can do this!"

The USO worked for weeks organizing the walkout. It was to be peaceful, yet powerful. Rameck, George, and Sampson all participated in the planning.

On a cool morning in April, at exactly the same time, hundreds of students from University High School quietly walked out of the building. They spilled onto the sidewalks and into the street. Some walked; some drove; some took busses to the Board of Education headquarters in downtown Newark. The buses and streets grew more crowded as, amazingly, students from Shabazz, Central, and other high schools joined the protest.

They locked arms and chanted. "We shall overcome!" they sang.

Police showed up and tried to stop them, but there were too many students to arrest. Besides, the students were peaceful, well behaved, and focused on their goal. Traffic was snarled as hundreds and hundreds of students marched toward the building.

"We want to speak to the superintendent!" Hassan and Ahi demanded of the timid-looking secretary who came out to greet them in the front of the building. "We have legitimate concerns, and we respectfully request a meeting to discuss them." The secretary scurried back inside with the message.

Of course, the superintendent refused to come out of his office. Students grew impatient and began pushing. A surge of students moved forward, and they entered the lobby of the building. They sat down and refused to move until someone came to speak to them. Hassan, the loudest and most outspoken, was arrested for disturbing the peace.

HE FELT GOOD ABOUT HIMSELF AND WHAT HE HAD ACCOMPLISHED.

Eventually, the superintendent, an assemblyman, and a state senator showed up and spoke to the crowd, but the students' requests weren't addressed specifically or seriously. Hours passed. Gradually, students began to leave. They had jobs to get to, or family responsibilities.

"I gotta go, Rameck," George said. "I can't miss work tonight."

"Do what you gotta do, man. I'm staying," Rameck said with a smile. "It just feels right, you know?"

"I'm outta here, too, man," Sampson said. "Good luck."

Rameck and about fifty others refused to leave the lobby of the building that night. The police set up a guard, more to protect them than to detain them. Someone ordered them pizza. A parent brought blankets. But the students stayed the night, emphasizing the importance of their demands.

The next morning they went home, feeling victorious. Over the next few weeks, a committee was formed to develop the first curriculum at University High School that included African-American and Hispanic history.

Rameck was a hero at school and was even on the news briefly. He felt good about himself and what he had accomplished.

But that didn't stop him from getting in trouble.

He didn't like his biology teacher. Something about the woman made him want to push her buttons. He'd ask questions in class that he already knew the answers to and do everything she asked the class not to do.

"Rameck, you forgot that these lab reports must be turned in with writing only on the front of the paper. You wrote on both sides."

"I'm saving trees," Rameck responded, a devilish smile on his face.

"You'll have to do it over if you want to get credit for it," the teacher whined.

"That would waste even more trees," Rameck said innocently. "Besides, every single answer on that paper is correct. Check them out."

"I refuse to grade a paper that has not been done according to the rules," the teacher insisted.

Rameck shrugged, balled up the assignment, and tossed it into the trash can. "Satisfied?" he asked. George and Sampson watched from their seats, laughing.

The teacher tensed but said nothing else. Rameck sat for the rest of the class, ignoring her, earphones on his head as he listened to music. The teacher did her best to ignore him.

A couple of days later, Rameck had skipped a class and was roaming the halls with George and Sampson. The trio spied a seventh-grade boy walking toward them. The kid carried a can of Silly String in his hand.

"Give me that!" Rameck demanded. "You want to get in trouble?" He was much bigger than the kid, and the very presence in the hall of a group of juniors was enough to make the boy toss the can to Rameck and scurry away in the other direction.

Rameck laughed and tossed the can from George to Sampson, with no particular purpose in mind. Suddenly he said, "Let's go see the biology teacher!" They ran down the empty hall to the teacher's room, then knocked on her locked door.

The door opened. The teacher stood there staring at the three friends. "What do you want?" she asked, seemingly angry that she had been interrupted.

Without a word, Rameck raised his hand, pushed the button of the aerosol can, and sprayed a sticky web of bright pink Silly String up, down, and across the astonished teacher's face.

In confusion, the teacher turned to her class. They cracked up, falling out of their chairs with hysterical laughter. The teacher was humiliated and furious. Rameck, knowing he had gone too far, disappeared down the hall.

"Rameck Hunt, please report to the principal's office!" the loudspeaker announced.

Rameck slipped into the office and held his breath while the principal yelled at him for being stupid, insubordinate, and thoughtless, all of which Rameck knew was true.

"You're suspended from school as of this moment, Rameck. Indefinitely," he added.

"You mean I can't come back—ever?" Rameck asked in disbelief. He thought about all his mother and grandmother had sacrificed for him, about the loss of friends, about how he really did like learning things, and he slumped down the hall and out of the door.

In the days that followed, the teacher developed an allergic reaction to the chemical in the Silly String and threatened to file criminal charges. The superintendent upheld Rameck's expulsion, and a final hearing was held. Rameck, dressed in a suit and tie and armed with an apology, waited to see his future crumble.

When asked to make a statement, Rameck stood and spoke. He looked directly at the teacher. "I'm really sorry for what I did. I wasn't thinking about consequences. Sometimes I do that—my mouth or my hands go off before my brain gets involved. Actually, I really like biology. I love science, and it's easy for me. I don't know what else to say except that I'm really, really sorry. I hope that one day you can forgive me."

The teacher, whose face was slightly swollen from the chemical reaction, said nothing and looked the other way. Rameck sat down, sure he was doomed to roam the streets of Newark, another dropout with nothing to do.

Then the teacher asked to speak. Inwardly, Rameck groaned. She walked with dignity to the front of the room. She did not look at Rameck, but spoke directly to the superintendent of Newark schools, the same man that Rameck and his friends had made demands of just a few weeks before.

"Don't expel him," she said quietly. Rameck looked up in surprise. "He's an over-enthusiastic teenager. Yes, he's thoughtless and foolish, but he's also one of the brightest students I have. Let him come back to school."

Rameck could not believe his ears. The superintendent, after a long and thoughtful deliberation, decided to listen to the teacher. Rameck was allowed to return to classes, a thankful, quieter, and more cooperative student—at least for a while.

FOOLISHNESS AND UNDERSTANDING

Silly String almost changed my life. That was a really foolish thing for me to do. I thought what I did was funny, and so did my friends. It kind of made me feel good, but while my friends were laughing, I was the one who got into big trouble. I never thought ahead to what might happen if I did something—I just acted on the first thought that came into my head, and that was usually a bad idea. It took a long time for me to learn that inappropriate activities always brought negative consequences. I certainly wasn't laughing when I was about to be kicked out of school.

I was very lucky. When I was in that meeting with my biology teacher, I thought it was over. I was really sorry, but, to be honest, I was most concerned about what would happen to me if I got kicked out of school. I wanted to take it back more than anything in the world. When she asked them to pardon me, I was very thankful. I also had a newfound respect for her. She wasn't as bad as I thought. Maybe she understood the thoughtless, impulsive behavior of kids more than I knew.

Sometimes, however, sudden decisions can be good if the results are positive. Our decision to protest what we believed to be an unfair practice in our school resulted in social awareness for a group of energetic teenagers and cultural improvement for our school. If I had spent more energy in high school trying to improve the lives of others instead of making a nuisance of myself, I might have learned a lot earlier the importance of making a positive difference in the world. ▪

CHAPTER TWELVE

"I THINK WE COULD ALL DO THIS— THE THREE OF US— TOGETHER!"

ELEVENTH GRADE "Yo, Rameck, you still gonna try out for the baseball team?" George asked. He and Sampson had played on the school's team since ninth grade. George played first base, while Sampson played shortstop and pitcher.

"Yeah, man, how hard can it be to out-hit the two of you?" Rameck replied with his usual grin. Rameck, somehow, had never played much baseball while he was a kid, but he was strong and athletic and figured he could learn just about any sport.

"Come to batting practice after school, and we'll make you eat that bat for dinner," Sampson joked. By this time Sampson had developed into a skillful, potentially professional baseball player. He was the captain of the baseball team at

University and could almost touch his dreams of playing in the major leagues. He often had write-ups in the local paper, highlighting his playing performance: "Davis goes three for four, with four RBIs, while pitching a four-hitter as University tops Shabazz 6–5." He knew, if he really worked at it, that he could get a baseball scholarship.

The three friends drove to a park that had batting cages and pitching machines that tossed the balls to the batter automatically. Rameck took his place, ready to bat.

"Keep your hands together," George shouted from the other side of the fence.

"Bend your knees a little," Sampson offered.

"I've watched the Yankees for years," Rameck said, ignoring both of them. "Baseball is easy!"

The machine pitched the first ball. Rameck swung with a powerful twist. He missed. The second ball erupted from the machine. Rameck swung again. He missed it by a mile. A third ball came. He swung and missed that one, too. The balls kept coming. Rameck kept swinging. And missing. George and Sampson, rolling with laughter, tried to offer suggestions at first to help him hit at least one of the balls. Finally, they gave up trying to help and just sat down on the ground, doubled over in laughter.

The machine finally ran out of balls, and Rameck stopped swinging. He looked at his friends, tossed the bat away, and had no choice but to laugh with them. When Sampson and George could catch their breath and had stopped their uncontrollable giggling, Rameck said, "Forget this. I'm better at playing girls than baseball any day. I think I'll just stick to what I know."

"Well, I hope you don't strike out with girls as many times as you struck out today," George said. That got them started again, and they laughed all the way home.

Sitting in Sampson's car later that night, the three of them got to talking about their futures, as they found themselves doing many times.

"You know we're almost out of this prison they call high school," Rameck said jokingly.

"It's not so bad," George said. "Some of the teachers are too easy, and some just don't care, but it's basically cool with me."

"What you gonna do when you graduate now that you're not getting kicked out?" Sampson asked Rameck.

"Well, I know Mrs. Silly String would never believe it, but I'd really like to be a teacher," Rameck admitted.

"So kids not even born yet can do to you what we did to our teachers?" Sampson asked with a laugh.

Rameck sighed. "No, 'cause I know what it's like to be a kid who needs more but doesn't know how to ask for it. Only a few teachers know how to reach out to kids like me. I could do that."

"You're right, man," George said. "But I don't want to teach—I want to be a doctor or nurse or something medical."

"I don't even know what you have to do to become something like that," Sampson said honestly.

COULD THIS BE THE CHANCE HE WAS LOOKING FOR — THE ANSWER TO THE QUESTIONS HE DIDN'T EVEN KNOW HOW TO ASK?

"I don't either," George said. "But I figure you need big piles of money and about a million years to spend in college."

"Hassan and Ahi are going to Howard University in D.C.," Rameck commented, "but their folks have a little cash." He fell silent.

"I think it would be cool to go into business," Sampson said. "You know, become an entrepreneur and own some big company." He sounded a little vague.

"What kind of business is there around here except for drugs and crime?" George asked bitterly.

"Show business!" Rameck told him. "We can be rap stars!"

"Yeah, right. You need money even to do that," Sampson told him.

Sampson drove the other two home then, their hopes and dreams left in the starlight.

The next day at school, bored and restless, Rameck, George, and Sampson sat in the back of their math class, making smart remarks and funny noises. The teacher looked up in exasperation. "You three clowns plan to make jokes the rest of your life?" she asked.

"Maybe," Sampson replied.

"You want to get out of this class?"

"Now that's no maybe. That's a definite yes!" George answered, laughing.

"Then the three of you get out of here. Colleges come to this school every day, looking for good students, and you three jokers let it all pass you by."

"College?" Rameck mumbled. "Too hard. Too long. Too much money." But he was interested, despite what he said.

"Right now, there's a presentation about Seton Hall University in the library. Go check it out," the teacher suggested.

"Anything to get out of here," Sampson said with a grin. The three of them got their books and headed out of the classroom, having no intention of going to the presentation.

"Let's go shoot some hoops, man," Rameck suggested.

"I'm with you, brother!" the other two replied. The three of them ran gleefully through the empty halls toward the gym.

"Where are you going, gentlemen?" the principal's loud, authoritarian voice boomed behind them.

They stopped and turned. "Uh, the library," George said, thinking quickly.

"The library is that way," the principal said without smiling. She pointed down the other hall.

"Thanks, ma'am," Sampson said as the three turned and headed back to the library. "We got lost." George and Rameck stifled their laughter.

"If you're looking for the Seton Hall presentation, it's just beginning," the principal told them. She walked with the three boys to the library, then stood by the door, listening to the presentation herself for a few minutes.

We're stuck, Sampson thought as the three of them found seats at a back table.

George said nothing. He had turned his attention to the speaker at the front of the room. "This sounds interesting."

"I am from Seton Hall University," the speaker began, "and we have a special program that some of you might find appealing. Did you know that there is a vast need for minorities in the health professions? Did you know that in this city alone, people have to wait for hours to see a doctor because there are not enough doctors on staff at the hospitals to see them?"

Sampson thought back to that day the stone fell on his foot and how the doctor with the magical X-rays had helped him heal properly.

Rameck thought back to the many times he had been taken to the emergency room for various scrapes and bruises.

George thought back to his many visits to the dentist and how fascinating the whole process had been for him.

"Seton Hall University," she continued, "is dedicated to training more minority students to enter medicine, not as aides and orderlies, although those are important jobs, but as *doctors*!" She paused for effect.

George felt his heart beating faster. Could this be the chance he was looking for—the answer to the questions he didn't even know how to ask?

"The Pre-Medical/Pre-Dental Plus program," she said, "is committed to help you prepare for study in a medical, dental, or other health-related field. It is funded by the State of New Jersey's Educational Opportunity Fund."

George raised his hand. "So how much does it cost?"

"Tuition and basic costs are covered. That's why this program is so selective and so worthwhile."

"You mean it's *free*?" he asked incredulously.

"Nothing is completely free, but we've got you covered for the large part of it," she replied with a laugh.

George sat there with a look of disbelief and possibility on his face. He asked another question. "How long does it take?"

"The program is a four-year undergraduate degree program.

Students must study a science major in the College of Arts and Sciences at Seton Hall University."

"So I can be a doctor in four years?" Rameck asked half-jokingly.

"Four years is just the undergraduate part," she replied. "Medical or dental school is another four-year program, plus additional years of study after that."

"That's an awfully long time," Rameck said, sitting down with defeat on his face.

"You'll be four years older whether you go to college or not. Why not fill up those four years with something valuable?" she shot back.

Rameck looked thoughtful but said nothing.

George thought back to Miss Johnson, who had said almost the exact same thing to him way back in third grade.

The Seton Hall representative continued, "You will receive academic, career, and personal counseling. An advisor will help you plan course work in preparation for advanced-level science courses."

"Some of that stuff is really hard. Suppose a person messes up?" Sampson asked.

"Tutoring in key science disciplines is offered at least two times per week—more if you need it. You're never alone. You have folks there who want to see you succeed."

"Is it guaranteed that we will get into medical and dental school after undergraduate studies?" Samspon asked.

"Pretty much, but you have to do well and work toward good grades."

"Deep," George mumbled. He was swallowing every word,

his excitement building as she continued to describe this unbelievable opportunity.

"Is it hard to get in this program?" a student asked.

"You have to have the grades, teacher recommendations, a personal interview, SAT scores—that sort of thing. But mostly you have to have the desire. Anything you want badly enough you can achieve."

Sampson and Rameck looked doubtful, but George's face was full of excitement.

"In addition," the woman said, "a seven-week summer program offers students courses in college-level chemistry, mathematics, and writing. These courses facilitate the transition to studying at the college level. Students earn up to seven undergraduate credits in the summer program."

"Summer school? On purpose?" Rameck looked doubtful.

"We find it really helps. The students get to know each other, learn about life on a college campus, and learn study skills that they might have skimmed over in high school."

Sampson looked at George and Rameck. The three of them were used to getting good grades with very little effort. Real studying and hard academic discipline were foreign to them.

The woman from Seton Hall finished her presentation, then handed out packets that included the application for the program. The students filed out slowly. George, Rameck, and Sampson stayed behind, not worrying about being late to their next class.

"What do you think?" George asked the other two.

"It's all right," Rameck said without conviction. "I still would rather go to Howard with Hassan and Ahi."

"Sounds like a possibility," Sampson added, "but I got to keep my options open. Besides, I still want to play college baseball, and I don't know much about their sports program."

But George would not give up. "Hey, look. I really want to do this. I think we could ALL do this—the three of us— together!"

"Maybe," Rameck said slowly.

"It's an awfully long time," Sampson said with a sigh.

"Man, we can go to college for FREE!" George said, trying to convince them.

"Free is always good," Rameck said with a grin.

"What do we have to lose? Let's just do the applications and see what happens," George suggested.

"Yeah, man—why not?" Sampson told the others. "Let's go for it."

Rameck added, "Can't hurt anything. Who knows—this might turn out to be a good thing."

They stuffed the applications into their backpacks and headed off to their next class. None of them was aware that their futures were enclosed in a folder stuck between a peanut butter sandwich, a chemistry lab homework assignment, and a pair of dirty gym shoes.

THE BEGINNING OF THE PACT

Thinking back to that presentation in the library makes me smile. What started out as three high school boys skipping class turned out to be the most significant event in our lives. If we had made it to the gym that day instead of the library, more than likely the streets would have swallowed us in the next few years. We never would have become doctors. Everything we needed to start on the road to success was included in one forty-five-minute presentation. And we almost missed it.

This was the first time that a path to my dreams was shown to me. Deep inside, I knew I could accomplish anything if given the chance. I just didn't know how to find that opportunity. That presentation showed me the possibility of reaching goals I had only dared to dream about. I think if a person dreams hard enough, sometimes a door will open to make that dream come true. Of course, it helps to be prepared to go through the door when the opportunity arises. We almost missed it.

We also had no idea that day that we were forming a pact that would last a lifetime. We just knew that somehow each of us individually might fail, but the strength of the three of us together just might be enough to succeed. ■

CHAPTER THIRTEEN

"IF HE DIES, YOU GET CHARGED WITH ATTEMPTED MURDER."

RAMECK, ELEVENTH GRADE "You need to quit hangin' with those thugs you run with," Rameck's mother said for the hundredth time. "You gonna end up in jail, just like your daddy!"

"But those are my boys!" Rameck replied defensively. "They always got my back."

"They're gonna end up puttin' your back in prison—or a cemetery!" his mother asserted. Rameck knew his mother was right, but his allegiance to his friends in the Plainfield neighborhood was too strong for even a mother to break up. It was just plain hard for Rameck, trying to figure out how to become a man in a place where manhood is measured differently than the way your mother sees it.

"I'll be back in a couple of hours," Rameck said as he

grabbed his black trench coat. It was the day before Thanksgiving, and the house was filled with the pleasant smells of turkey gravy and apple pie, but he was a little angry that she kept at him for things over which he had no control. He left the house then and headed down the street. The day was chilly and blustery. He ended up where he always hung out—on the back steps of the closed and dreary Clinton Elementary School, sitting with his friends, sharing a forty-ounce bottle of Old English Malt Liquor. They had no particular plan or purpose.

"Yo, man, look at that crackhead heading this way. Makes me sick the way they be hanging around all the time," Rameck said with disgust as the man, skinny and very high, stumbled toward them.

"Didn't he used to be a lifeguard down at the swimming pool?" a dude named Train asked.

"Yeah, man, but crack don't care who you are or who you used to be," Rameck replied.

The crack addict, with matted hair; red, glassy eyes; and filthy clothes, said in a thin, raspy voice, "Let me cop a rock off y'all."

Rameck and his friends tried to ignore him, but the junkie would not give up. "Come on, now. I know one of y'all can hook a brother up."

Train, who actually had some crack to sell, told the addict, "I'll sell it to you, man, but you can't smoke it here. Got that?" Rameck knew what he meant. There was a generally understood rule in the neighborhood that the school grounds were off limits for drugs. Little kids hung out there, and Rameck and his friends felt like they were protecting the younger generation, even if it meant just in this one small area. It was a matter of pride, a code of honor, an unwritten law of the streets.

The crackhead nodded shakily, gave Train the money, and stumbled away. A few minutes later, Rameck looked up and saw the orange-and-blue glare of a crack pipe blazing from behind a Dumpster in the school yard.

"I told him not to do that mess around here," Train said angrily. "I ought to go beat his butt."

As if on cue, Rameck, Train, and the other boys put down their bottles and walked over to the Dumpster. Train yelled at the crackhead, "I thought I told you, man. You don't be smokin' that stuff around here!"

"I'm sorry. I'm sorry. I'm sorry," the trembling crackhead replied, cowering from Train's anger.

"So raise up on out of here. We want you out of here right now!" Train insisted. "Get outta here!"

"Hold on, let me just finish," the addict said weakly. He put his lips around the crack pipe and inhaled deeply. His eyes were still closed when Train punched him. The addict fell to his knees.

Liquor and adrenaline took over. Rameck and his friends began beating the man. "You dropped him, man," one of them shouted as he hit the helpless addict.

"Let's knock his lights out. Useless crackhead," yelled another.

The man stumbled back to his feet. Somebody else hit him again and knocked him back down. He moaned, writhing in pain on the ground.

Rameck and his friends were out of control. Rameck lifted the man up, not to help him, but so he'd be a better target. They hit him again. And again. For fifteen or twenty minutes they beat the man until he could barely move. Their anger at the man made no sense, but somehow he represented all the drugs, all the death, all the sorrow they saw on the streets every day, and their pent-up rage exploded all over the man's body.

Suddenly Rameck reached into the pocket of his trench coat and pulled out a small switchblade. "Check this out!" he said with bravado as he waved the knife in the air.

The looks of awe and admiration on the faces of his friends encouraged him, but Rameck was suddenly afraid. Afraid to use the knife and afraid not to use it. He jabbed the man in the thigh, hoping inwardly that he had not really injured him. He slipped the knife back into his pocket, trying to appear as cool as the look on the faces of his friends as they admired his courage.

They left the man lying on the sidewalk, bruised and bleeding. Calmly, they walked to the store, bought three candy bars, then sauntered back to the parking lot of the school. It didn't occur to Rameck that anyone would care about the beaten drug addict until he heard the siren of a police car. He was genuinely surprised.

MANY SEEMED TO ACCEPT JAIL AS PART OF THEIR LIFE, AS THEIR INEVITABLE FUTURE. BUT RAMECK BRISTLED AT THE THOUGHT.

"What we gonna do?" Rameck asked. "Should we run?"

"Just play it cool," Train said. "They ain't got nothing on us."

A police officer approached them. Rameck's heart thudded, but he pretended to look bored.

"We got a report that some dudes who fit your description beat up someone pretty bad," he said.

"It wasn't us," Rameck told him.

"The man who got beat up said one of you was wearing a black trench coat and had a knife," the officer said.

Rameck felt his knees go weak. The policeman made him stand up and patted him down. He missed the knife. Rameck gave a sigh of relief.

Then a second officer said, "Let me pat this one down again."

"I ain't got no knife!" Rameck yelled. "Your buddy already checked me out."

The policeman ignored him. "You better not be lying to me, boy."

"I ain't lying!" Rameck was trembling with fear.

Slowly and carefully the second officer frisked Rameck. He whispered in Rameck's ear, "If I find a knife, I'm gonna hurt you." He found the knife.

"I told you not to lie to me!" the officer said angrily. He threw Rameck against the police car, then kneed him in the stomach. Rameck groaned in pain and anger and fear as he was handcuffed.

The crack addict, who was being wheeled into an ambulance by now, looked up and identified Rameck, Train, and the others as the ones who had assaulted him.

Rameck and his friends were tossed into the back of a police car and taken down to the station. Rameck, who just a couple of hours ago had left a home full of the soothing smells of Thanksgiving dinner, was stuck in the back of a police car that smelled vaguely of sweat, urine, and disinfectant.

"That crackhead you beat up is critically injured," a policeman told them when they arrived at the station. "He may die."

Rameck shuddered in fear. "What does that mean?" he managed to ask.

The policeman didn't blink an eye. "If he dies, you get charged with attempted murder."

"Oh, my God," Rameck whispered to himself. "Please don't let this man die."

"You want to call your mother?" the officer asked.

Rameck nodded, called his mother, and tried to explain to her what had happened. "We didn't mean to hurt him. We just got carried away!" he said to her. He knew it sounded weak.

"Well, why don't you just think about that for a while," his mother snapped back.

"You're not gonna come get me?" he asked.

"No, I'm not. You sit there for a while and see what jail is really like. Maybe this will teach you a lesson." She hung up the phone.

Rameck was taken, in handcuffs, to a detention center in a nearby town. His mother, who decided at the last minute to come and rescue him, got there too late. Since it was a holiday weekend, Rameck would be forced to stay in jail until Monday.

He was placed in a cell with two other boys he didn't know. The cell consisted of a toilet and two cots, both of which were occupied, so the officer told him to sleep on the floor. On Thanksgiving morning, instead of waking up in his own bed to the smells of Thanksgiving and the sound of football games and parades, Rameck woke stiffly on the cold concrete floor of a jail cell.

He spent four days in that detention center. He ate terrible food; endured embarrassment and humiliation as he used the toilet in front of his cellmates; and even heard, late one night, the horrifying but unmistakable sounds of a boy being raped. Rameck felt like a caged animal.

Some of the boys in the jail had been there many times. Many seemed to accept jail as part of their life, as their inevitable future. But Rameck bristled at the thought. "Never again," he told himself. "I'm not going to waste my life this way."

When he was released, he was at first ashamed to tell George and Sampson what had happened. The three of them talked about football games and girls and applying to Seton Hall as if the world were unchanged. But Rameck's fear of what might happen to his future shaded everything.

In January, he attended a hearing before a judge. Several teachers and family members had written letters on his behalf, asking for mercy. The crack addict did not show up, however, so the case was continued. A second hearing was held. Once again, the addict did not show up. A third hearing was set. Rameck, dressed in his suit and tie, waited for the worst to happen. But again, the man they attacked did not appear in court. The judge finally threw out the case, and after several stern warnings from all involved, Rameck was allowed to go home.

"Thank, you, God," Rameck whispered. He felt as if he had been racing blindfolded to the edge of a cliff and had been grabbed and saved just as he was about to descend into a pit from which there was no escape.

He swore he'd try to stay out of trouble, to hang with Sampson and George more, aim for higher goals. For a while, it worked.

THANKSGIVING IN JAIL

Waking up in jail was a surreal experience. That first morning I honestly thought I was having a bad dream. When I opened my eyes and realized I wasn't dreaming, I was terrified. I had gotten myself into a big mess, and it was horrible. I had almost taken the life of another human being. How could I have been so heartless and cruel?

That experience taught me so much. I learned up close about all the horrible things that happen to people in jail. Beatings. Stabbings. Rapes. The next thing I learned took me by surprise. I realized I wasn't free. I looked out of the window and saw all of the people going about their daily lives and realized I wasn't able to do that. I couldn't go to school, I couldn't go to the store, and I couldn't get a bite to eat at the local takeout. All I had were stale milk and processed turkey for that Thanksgiving meal. I had given up on my chance to make choices and freely decide what I wanted to do each day. It was stifling.

Finally, I came to a realization while I was in that jail that changed my life forever. When I looked around at everyone there with me, I realized none of them was thinking about freedom or choices or even the bad food. They were resigned to this life, as if that was how life was supposed to be. They had no goals, no future outside of those jail walls. That disgusted me most of all.

With all of that, I prayed to God and asked for forgiveness. I told Him that if He got me out of this mess, I would never be back again, and I never was. It took me some time to get my act all the way together, but after that experience I was well on my way. ∎

CHAPTER FOURTEEN

"HOW DO YOU PLEAD?" THE JUDGE ASKED. "GUILTY, YOUR HONOR."

SAMPSON, TWELFTH GRADE It was the summer between junior and senior year. School was out, and Sampson, glad to be away from homework and teachers and academic responsibilities for a little while, enjoyed kicking it with his friends on the corner.

They knew the most dangerous thing to do in Newark was to stand on the corner and mind your own business. Anything could happen—a drive-by shooting, a fight, police harassment. The corner was the welcome center for all of it. Nevertheless, that is where they hung out every day.

Sampson had been warned many times by his mother to stay off of the corner. "There is nothing but trouble out there. Whatever happened to you hanging out with Reggie? You need to get back into kung fu. Those boys you hang out with now aren't going anywhere with their life. Remember, you make your bed, you got to lay in it!"

Sampson knew his mother was right. She had been through so many struggles, and he realized that she wanted a better life for him. She tried to keep him on a straight path, but the streets were getting the best of him. Aimless summer days, with nothing to do, were the biggest opportunity for him to fall into trouble and become another statistic.

George and Rameck had jobs that summer, so the three friends did not spend as much time together during vacation, and Sampson fell back into old habits with old friends. He found work at McDonald's, which gave him spending money, but little else. The desire to have more and to have it quickly was overpowering in a neighborhood where drug dealers drove expensive cars and walked around decorated in diamonds and gold as commonly as trees wore leaves of green.

"Man, I need to make a move," Sampson said, flexing his muscles and stretching his neck. He felt like a toy wound up too tightly. "Got any ideas?"

"Rob somebody before they rob you," joked a kid named Buddy.

"Hey, you got a good idea there, man. Why don't we rob some drug dealers? They got plenty of cash," another dude suggested.

"You crazy, man? They got guns and will shoot you dead before you have a chance to spend a dime of their money," Sampson said.

"No, man," Buddy said. We don't rob the experienced drug dudes—we hit the young ones, the stupid ones, the kids."

"Yeah, sounds like a plan to me," another boy in their group said. "We hit them hard, hit them quick, then get out of there before they know what happened."

Sampson was doubtful it would work, but it sounded so easy. It wasn't wrong, he figured—they wouldn't be selling any drugs, just taking money away from kids who *did* sell the stuff. They would be like the Robin Hoods of their community by taking from those who were poisoning the area.

The first couple of times they tried it, everything went smoothly. Sampson and his boys dressed all in black and drove to a street corner where they knew drug dealers hung out. One of the boys always pulled out a gun to scare the kids into obedience. Sampson didn't like the inclusion of the gun in the process because he felt it increased their chances of things going wrong. The last thing Sampson needed was for someone to get shot in all the chaos. Nonetheless, a gun was simply part of the scene, as natural to him and his friends as pulling out a candy bar from a pocket.

Sampson and his friends would snatch the money from the unsuspecting young dealers and jump back into their car before anyone had a chance to respond. They split the money four ways and exulted in the ease and glory of it all. Nobody ever got hurt.

The next time they went out, Sampson was the driver. Even though somewhere deep down he felt uncomfortable about what they were doing, the excitement of the attack and the exhilaration of the take were too much to resist.

They drove around until they spotted a group of teenagers hanging out on a corner. They knew the kids there had to be dealers. Sampson, Buddy, and the other two boys jumped out of Sampson's car, preparing to beat up the kids. Buddy pulled out a gun. "Empty your pockets!" he demanded harshly.

Usually when they did this, the kids they jumped gave Sampson and his friends their money and ran away. But this time, just as the kids were fearfully handing over the money, another car—a brown, four-door Chevrolet—unexpectedly pulled up next to them. In that car were four older dudes, heavier and tougher-looking than the kids they were used to dealing with. They looked at Sampson and his friends suspiciously.

Sampson saw with alarm that the car had a police radio mounted on the floor. "Cops!" he shouted wildly to his friends, each of whom took off running.

Suddenly police cars appeared from all directions, sirens blaring, lights flashing. Instead of running, Sampson walked slowly, appearing to be unfazed by the commotion. No one stopped him. He kept walking, hoping and praying that he would get away. Finally he made it to the corner and began to run—huge, loping strides that took him blocks away from the scene.

When he got far enough away, he stopped, caught his breath, and wiped the sweat from his brow. He waited a half hour or so, then doubled back to the scene to pick up his car.

"No one from our neighborhood ever makes it out. You either are gunned down, or arrested, or you get some crazy disease."

It was gone. There was no trace of the dealers, the police, or the crowds of people who had gathered to watch the excitement. The street corner was deserted.

Not sure what to do, Sampson hailed a cab and went home. He told no one what had gone down that afternoon, and he slept very little that night, worrying about what would happen when was his name was connected to that car.

The next morning, he made some calls and found that his car had been towed by the Montclair police department. They asked him to come in for questioning. All three of the boys he'd been with the day before had been arrested.

Sampson finally confided in his older sister, who drove him to the police station. "They'll probably let you go, since you're a juvenile," she said with a confidence that Sampson didn't share.

Sampson sat in silence, playing the scene over and over again in his mind. He was stuck on the same point—had they connected him to the robbery?

When they arrived at the station, Sampson was taken into a small, dark room inside the police headquarters. In it were a table and two chairs. Sampson sat down on one side of the table. A detective sat down on the other and flipped on a tape recorder. Sampson trembled inside, but he didn't show it.

"People say you were involved in an incident yesterday," the detective began.

"What incident was that?" Sampson replied, appearing clueless.

"Marshall," the officer said, "you might as well come clean.

Your boys already told us the whole story." Sampson took a deep breath, realizing it had to be true. The detective had called him by his middle name, Marshall. Only his family and friends knew Sampson by that name. Sampson thought about the code of the streets. What happened to the loyalty, the no-snitch policy? How dare they rat on him?

The detective interrupted Sampson's thoughts and began to describe the robbery. Sampson still considered lying, pretending to know nothing about what had happened, but it was too late for that now. He had been caught and had to tell the truth. For the first time, Sampson realized that the streets had no love for him.

Sampson sighed and said, "Yeah, I was there. But we didn't hurt nobody."

"Did you take their money?"

"It was drug money."

"I repeat, did you take the money?"

"Yes, sir."

"Did one of you have a gun?"

"I never touched the gun," Sampson declared.

"I repeat, did one of you have a gun?"

"Yes, sir." Sampson slumped in his chair in defeat. He thought, *I knew that gun would get us in trouble.*

"I'm placing you under arrest. Because a gun was involved in the commission of this crime, you are being charged with armed robbery and will be sent to a juvenile detention center in Newark."

"I can't go home?" Sampson asked. "My sister said since I was a juvenile, I'd be released."

"Your sister was wrong."

Sampson was taken to the detention center—a nice name for a jail. It had four units, based on the type of crime committed. Sampson was placed in Unit One, the section where juveniles arrested for violent crimes were assigned. Even the word *crime* stuck in his throat. What they had done was just for fun, something to do to take up time during the hot summer. He had never considered it a crime. But the police certainly did.

How did I get myself in a place like this? he thought miserably. *How could I let down my parents, the rest of my family? What am I going to tell Rameck and George?* He did not know at that time that Rameck had been in a similar situation just a few months before. All he knew was that he had never felt so alone, so out of place, and so angry with himself.

He had lots of time to think as he lay awake those hot summer nights, unable to sleep on the hard cot in the skinny, uncomfortable cell. It was tiny, with barely enough space to fit a body in. He had no pillow or blanket, not even a sheet to cover him. The thin mattress had been slept on by many previous bodies and was decorated with saturated urine stains from former residents.

The boys he'd been arrested with had also been incarcerated, but for some reason, not at the location where Sampson was held. He didn't know where they were, and he didn't care. They had ratted him out and left him to suffer the consequences alone. Sampson resolved that if he ever got out, he'd stay away from dudes like that, but he knew it would be difficult.

He wondered how George and Rameck were spending their

summer. He thought quite a bit about the plans they had made together to try for the program at Seton Hall. Years of college or years of jail? There was no comparison.

Sampson had once asked George, who always seemed focused on the goal of making it to college, how he did it. "I just believe it can happen," George had said.

"But how?" Sampson had insisted. "It just seems easier to give up. No one from our neighborhood ever makes it out. You're either gunned down, or arrested, or you get some crazy disease. Everybody fails," he had declared.

"But I don't plan to fail," George had replied with a grin. Sampson let the subject drop. Here in this hot jail cell, failure walked with him every day. It was difficult to see a bright outcome.

His parents visited him regularly and hired a lawyer. Sampson felt bad that he had to face his parents in that kind of setting, where they could visit him only for limited periods of time. It hurt him that he had caused them so much pain.

"What has the lawyer told you lately?" Sampson asked his mother during one visit.

"They're talking about trying you as an adult," his mother said with fear in her voice. "That means a possible sentence of three to ten years in an adult prison!"

"Three to ten years! Are they crazy?" Sampson replied.

Sampson was terrified at the thought of being locked up for so long. Just the few weeks he had spent in the detention center were more time than he ever wanted to do.

Each day took an eternity to pass by. The routines were strict, the food was awful, and the other residents seemed to function as one mindless organism. Sampson did his best to keep himself

George (back, center) and friends strike a pose.

(below, right) Rameck in junior high
(below, left) Sampson and his friend Frank
hanging out in Newark, summer 1988

(left) Sampson and Rameck at University High School

(below) George and Rameck in the chemistry lab

Sampson, George, and Rameck became friends at University High School. By the time they graduated in 1991, they had all been accepted into Seton Hall's Pre-Medical/Pre-Dental Plus Program. They made a pact to support each other through all the years of school ahead of them on the path to becoming doctors.

(above) Sampson takes a moment to shake a friend's hand during the graduation march.

(below) George picks up his prom date.

(above) **Sampson chillin' in the dorm room**

(right) **Rameck studying**

Sampson, George, and Rameck spent seven weeks in the summer program at Seton Hall, which offered students courses in college-level chemistry, mathematics, and writing.

(above) George, Sampson, and Rameck with their University High School math teacher, Mr. Davis (far left), at a banquet celebrating the completion of the summer course

(below) Sampson (left), friends Reagan, Gerald, Mike, and George (right) hanging out in the freshman dorm at Seton Hall

(*above*) Rameck, George, and Sampson, now the Three Doctors, after graduating from the School of Medicine and Dentistry of New Jersey in 1999

(*below*) Sampson, George, and Rameck with Carla Dixon, the student development specialist who supported them through their years at Seton Hall

(Photo © David Hollander/Photographic Services)

The Three Doctors have been honored with many awards, including an Essence
Lifetime Achievement Award in 2000. (Photo © Linz Photography)

The Three Doctors today

Rameck Hunt, M.D., is a board-certified internist at St. Peter's University Hospital and an assistant clinical professor of medicine at Robert Wood Johnson Medical School.

George Jenkins, D.M.D., is a faculty member of Community Health at the University of Medicine and Dentistry of New Jersey.

Sampson Davis, M.D., is a board-certified emergency-medicine physician at East Orange General Hospital and St. Michael's Medical Center, and a consultant for the Violence Prevention Institute focusing on gang awareness and preventive medicine in Essex County, New Jersey.

apart from their indifference. In the television room he watched the same shows over and over again while listening to the activities outside his window. Sometimes he sat at the window, trying to connect a face to the voices outside. A metal fence prevented him from seeing anyone on the ground level.

The lawyer worked furiously to get the charges lessened. Just before Sampson was scheduled to go to court, the lawyer told him that he had worked out a possible deal. "If you plead guilty as a juvenile, you'll get a two-year suspended sentence and two years of probation."

"What does that mean?" Sampson asked, unsure of the details of the legal system. "Will I have a record?"

"Not if we are able to get this plea agreement."

"I don't want to say I did something that I didn't do. I admit I did some stuff I shouldn't have, but for real, I never touched that gun," Sampson insisted.

The lawyer replied, "If you stay out of trouble—and I mean squeaky clean, you hear me—then you won't have to serve any time in jail. And since you are still a juvenile, the crime won't appear on your permanent record."

Sampson breathed deeply with relief.

Since this plea agreement had been pulled together at the very last minute, there had been no time to inform Sampson's parents. They knew nothing about it.

Sampson stood before the judge. His mother sat not far from him, behind the wooden partition.

"How do you plead?" the judge asked.

"Guilty, Your Honor," Sampson said. His heart thudded, and his mouth felt like it was full of cotton.

"Then it is the judgment of this court to sentence you to two years' suspended sentence and two years' probation, dependent upon . . ."

He was interrupted just then by a scream from the room. Sampson's mother, who thought the judge was sentencing her son to two years in jail, cried out, "Your Honor, take me instead! He's just a boy. He didn't know what he was doing. Oh, Lord, take me instead!"

At that moment, Sampson had never loved his mother more, and he realized for the first time how deeply she loved him. He felt ashamed and promised himself to turn his life around. Eventually everything was explained to her. The judge admonished Sampson about staying out of trouble, for his mother's sake, if for no other reason. After having spent four weeks in jail, Sampson was released. He swore to himself once more, *Never again. Never.*

A few weeks later, Sampson stood by the basketball hoops at Dayton Street School. Buddy, one of the other guys who'd been involved in the robbery, bounced the basketball. He was out on bail, awaiting his trial.

"What's up, man?"

"Chillin'," Sampson replied.

"You get off?" Buddy asked.

"Suspended sentence."

"You lucky. Helps that you're not eighteen yet," Buddy replied. He was older, had two prior offenses, and was going to do time in jail. They shot a few hoops. "So what you gonna do now?" Buddy asked.

"I'm thinking about going to college," Sampson said with pride. "Me and my partners from high school made a pact and have been talking about it."

Buddy and a couple of other guys who were shooting hoops with them stopped the game and broke down laughing. They laughed so hard they had to catch their breath. "Man, that ain't never gonna happen!" Buddy said. "Nobody from around here goes to college! Do you know who you are and where you from?"

Sampson said firmly, "Well, I will be the first." In that moment he realized he had to look beyond them, beyond their ridicule, and find a way to make it past the impossibilities. He left them laughing. That was the last time Sampson hung out with his boys.

Eventually, all of the boys who had been involved with Sampson in the robbery received jail time. Sampson had been spared for some reason he did not yet understand. But he was ready to find out.

NEVER AGAIN

There are turning points in everyone's life. My experience as a juvenile in the detention center helped me realize that I was traveling down a road of destruction. That summer helped me turn my life around and aim for something positive. I realized the company you keep plays tremendously in the outcome of your life. My street friends had given up and had no direction. I knew if I continued to hang out with them, I would fall victim to the same aimlessness.

Going to college was not a common goal for kids in my neighborhood. I felt I had no choice, however. College represented hope. Staying on the streets most likely meant more jail time or drug addiction or death. So I stepped out on faith and headed for a brighter future.

Often I felt survivor's guilt, since I left my family and neighborhood friends behind, but I realized before I can help anyone else, I must take care of myself first. Then I could reach out and give back. I feel strongly that giving back is a responsibility for all to embrace.

Let me tell you about the boys I used to hang out with. Two of them were murdered. Two of them are strung out on drugs. One of them is in jail. I have lost contact with the others.

And, yes, I held true to my promise—never again did I get involved with criminal activities. Never again did I get mixed up with the police. Never again did I travel on that road to destruction. ■

CHAPTER FIFTEEN

"NOT ONLY HAD THEIR SONS SURVIVED, BUT THEY WERE HEADING TO COLLEGE."

THE END OF HIGH SCHOOL "We better get in," Sampson said to George and Rameck.

"Hey, man, all three of us will get in. I'm sure of it," Rameck replied.

"We're in this together," George reminded them as he and Rameck worked on their applications for Seton Hall one afternoon in the school library. "It's gonna happen." They were seniors, getting close to graduation, full of both brash confidence and hidden fears.

"Yeah, you right, man. If it hadn't been for our pact, I might not have even tried for this," Sampson admitted. "But I ain't gonna let you two jokers get some free education and leave me on the streets to sell pencils!"

"What did you put on page three, question seven?" Rameck asked as he chewed on a pencil.

"Oh, the question about money saved in a bank account? I put 'Ain't got none!'" Sampson replied with a laugh. "The last time I saw the inside of a bank was when they were giving out free cookies to promote their new services." He sighed then. "I think we got a chance at doing this," he said seriously. "We have an opportunity to be something in life."

"I have a feeling this is right for us, man," George replied.

"How you get to be so positive and sure about stuff all the time, man?" Rameck asked him.

"I don't know. I just believe it can happen. One of us might fail if he tried to do this alone. Three of us together just can't be beat."

"Well, I'm still applying to Howard, too," Rameck said. "I gotta have a backup plan, and I hate to leave my boys Hassan and Ahi."

"I'm mailing my application to Seton Hall tomorrow," George announced.

"I mailed mine yesterday," Sampson told them.

"Well, if that's the case, then I better get mine in, too," Rameck said. "The applications from the three of us will blow everybody else right off the table!"

They laughed and headed out to their next class. Partly from the spirit of their pact and partly from their fear of failure, the three used each other as crutches when one felt weak, as tools when another needed information, and as weapons to face the future together as they headed into the unknown.

In the following weeks, each of them was called to Seton

> " IF THERE ARE THREE OF US,
> WE WON'T FEEL SO ALONE, AND WE'LL
> HAVE EACH OTHER FOR SUPPORT
> IF WE MESS UP. "

Hall, located in South Orange, a wealthy suburb of New Jersey, for an in-depth personal interview.

George was called first. He and his mother found their way through what seemed to be a huge campus, full of large brick buildings and perfectly kept lawns, to the office of Carla Dickson, the student development specialist for the program. Barely five feet tall, with a warm, smiling, brown face, she seemed much larger to George as he sat down in her tiny office.

"Why do you want to be a doctor, George?" she asked.

"I've always had this hidden desire to do something in medicine," George admitted earnestly. "Ever since my first visit to the dentist—I've had major dental work—I've thought being a dentist would be the best job in the world!" He grinned, a dreamy look of hopefulness on his face.

"And if you become a dentist, what then?" she asked.

"I'd like to start a clinic in Newark, I think. Lots of folks where I grew up didn't have access to good dental care, so they just ignored their teeth until it was too late. I'd like to help fix that problem."

Carla scribbled furiously on her notes, nodding with approval. "The program encourages the minority doctors we train to return to urban communities to work," she told George. "I'm impressed."

George breathed a sigh of relief and relaxed as he answered questions about grades and baseball and high school. "You know, I have two friends who have applied to this program also," George told her.

"Oh, really?" Carla replied.

"Yeah. We've kinda made a pact with each other to help us make it—a little like a support system for three. We figure that if there are three of us, we won't feel so alone, and we'll have each other for support if we mess up."

Again Carla scribbled and nodded vigorously. "This is very good," she said, almost to herself. She asked for the names of Rameck and Sampson and made more notes on George's application. She then stood up, shook George's hand, and thanked him for coming. "It will take several weeks to process all the applications," she told him. "But you will be informed of your acceptance or rejection before school gets out in June."

George left her office feeling confident and hopeful. Sampson and Rameck had their interviews with Carla in the next few days. Each of them mentioned the other two in their interviews, although none of them knew it at the time.

On a warm Friday morning in early April, Sampson walked into the senior homeroom carrying an envelope. He looked at George and Rameck and smiled.

"I got my letter from Seton Hall," he said.

"Did you get in?" George asked.

"I don't know. I didn't open it."

"You mean you had the thing since yesterday and you haven't opened it?" George asked. "I got my letter yesterday, too, and I opened it right away."

"Well, did you make it?" Rameck asked.

George looked triumphant. "Sure did!" Then he looked at the other two, afraid perhaps that they had not been accepted. "What about you, Rameck?"

Rameck grinned. "I'm in like sin! But I also got accepted to Howard yesterday." He looked a little confused. "But if all three of us get accepted, I think I'll go to Seton Hall with you two. We made a pact, didn't we?" The other two nodded seriously.

"Well, open the letter, Sam!" George and Rameck said at the same time. Sampson slowly opened the envelope, unfolded the letter, and read it. Then he refolded it and replaced it in the envelope.

"What did it say, Sam?" George asked.

"I'm not telling."

George and Rameck proceeded to tackle him to get the letter out of his hand. "OK! OK! I got in! Of course I got in!"

The three friends looked at each other with exhilaration and satisfaction as the bell rang for the first class of that day. "Now what?" Rameck asked, suddenly serious.

"We figure it out as it happens, I guess," George said.

"The part that makes it not so scary is that we figure it out together," Sampson added.

The rest of the school year disappeared in a flash. Last-minute school projects. Prom. Parties. On graduation day, dressed in burgundy caps and gowns, Rameck Hunt, Sampson Davis, and George Jenkins marched proudly down the aisle to the thunderous applause of their parents and friends. Cameras flashed. Speeches were made. Families cheered as the names of their children were called. These students were the success stories, the ones who had not dropped out or ended up in jail or strung out on drugs. These graduates were the results of much prayer and hope and just plain luck. Parents wept with thankfulness. The families of Sampson, George, and Rameck were especially proud that day. Not only had their sons survived the streets of Newark, but they were heading to college and planning to become doctors, a dream most kids could barely imagine. Caps were thrown into the air, and then it was suddenly over.

STRENGTHENING THE PACT

When I learned that we were all accepted into the program at Seton Hall, a tremendous weight was lifted from my shoulders. I was terrified at the thought of facing the uncertainties of college and the difficulties of higher education all by myself. I think some of my constant pushing and encouraging of Rameck and Sam was based more on my own fear than on my confidence.

Still, something inside me told me there was no obstacle that the three of us could not get through together. I'm not sure I would have made it without their friendship, support, and positive influence. I'm sure they feel the same way.

We made a pact, a promise, to each other to pull when one of us felt down, to push when one of us needed encouragement, and to stand by each other no matter what difficulties we encountered. That pact changed our lives.

You can do the same thing, you know. If you can find just one person who believes in himself or herself, who believes in a future with hope and possibility, who shares your desire to make it, hook up with that person and work together to reach your goals. Create your own pacts to succeed and stick together. It changed our lives. Perhaps it can do the same for you. ■

CHAPTER SIXTEEN

"IT FEELS GOOD, MAN. IT'S LIKE DOING PUSH-UPS WITH MY BRAIN!"

PRE-COLLEGE SUMMER PROGRAM "Well, no summer jobs for us this year," Rameck said as he tossed a pair of gym shoes into a suitcase.

George and Sampson had already finished packing. They were all leaving the next day for seven weeks on the Seton Hall campus to participate in a remediation and preparation program required for all students accepted into the Pre-Medical/Pre-Dental Plus program.

"You know, only ten people got accepted into the program this year," George commented. "There won't be much chance of slipping out of class unnoticed."

"That's cool. The three of us are together. Man, college! Who would have thought it?" Rameck said with feeling.

"You sorry you're not going to Howard, Rameck?" Sampson asked.

"Hey, man, Seton Hall is free. Howard costs money. Free is always a good choice. Besides, you're gonna need me if you decide to play some hoops on the weekends," he replied with a laugh.

"Yeah, you better bring your A game. I have some new moves I can show the both of you," Sampson said. "Besides, I have to stay in shape. Tryouts for the baseball team are this fall."

When they got to the campus, they were pleasantly surprised by their dormitory rooms. Each air-conditioned and carpeted room had two beds, a telephone, and a desk.

"Cool!" Rameck whispered as he tossed his stuff on the bed on the left. He roomed with Sampson. George had been placed in a room right across the hall, with another one of the students in the program.

The next morning at seven, the program began with full intensity. Carla Dickson stood in front of the group and said boldly, "You are doctors. Do you hear me? You are doctors. You have to believe it to achieve it. Never forget what you really are. Doctors. All doctors begin by knowing nothing. They study. They learn. They prepare. And they achieve their goals. So believe it, ladies and gentlemen. You ARE doctors! Believe it and achieve it." She said nothing more, but began to pass out the schedule of classes for the week.

Sampson, George, and Rameck looked at each other across the classroom and grinned. No one had ever given them such affirmation before. No one had ever given them permission to dream so large or to visualize the possibility of success.

They were scheduled for precalculus, biology, chemistry, computer skills, English, and critical-thinking courses. The courses were intense and demanding, with no tolerance for the sloppy work and careless attitudes of high school.

"You can do better, Rameck," one professor told him, so he did. No one had ever pushed him like that before.

"You will not miss an assignment, Sampson!" another professor insisted. Sampson accepted the challenge and never missed one.

Classes lasted every day until five, and after dinner they went to required tutoring sessions, where each student got help in areas of need. Their test scores began to rise. In the evening the students were required to study. No television was allowed during study hours, and bedtime was mandatory at ten P.M., which none of them liked very much.

"This feels like boot camp," Sampson whispered to Rameck one night after lights out.

"Yeah, but it feels good, man. It's like doing push-ups with my brain!"

"Wow. Doctors. Imagine us as physicians! I think we can do this," Sampson replied.

"I don't know, man. It seems like a pretty tall mountain to climb. But I didn't expect to be even close to the mountain, so who knows what's gonna happen," Rameck admitted.

"Carla's cool, though. She makes it seems like we can do this. It's like we are her three sons—her personal challenge and responsibility. I like the fact that she cares and believes in us."

"You sure can't get away with any stuff around her," Rameck said. "She's like a little dynamo. She's here before we get up, and she stays a long time after classes are over. She told me she's determined to see all three of us make it through."

"Yeah, she told me the same thing." Sampson chuckled. "She said that helping the three of us make it, even when we think we can't, is one of her own personal goals."

"I'm scared not to do what she says," Rameck replied with a laugh. "That little bitty thing might bite me in the kneecaps!"

A couple of weeks later, after Rameck had complained about the rigors of the program one too many times for Carla, she stopped him after class.

"You know what your problem is, Rameck?" she said angrily.

"No, but I bet you're going to tell me," he replied with a smile that tried to melt a little of her anger.

"You're just plain lazy! You think this is hard? Wait until you're pulling twenty-four-hour shifts as a resident in a hospital. Wait until you hold someone's life in your hands and that person is depending on YOU to have the skill and knowledge to save his life." She whipped back into her lecturing voice. "Strict personal discipline and adherence to rules are absolutely necessary for a doctor's success!" She glared at him.

"I'm not lazy," Rameck replied sullenly. "I'm just not used to all this discipline."

No one had ever given them permission to dream so large or to visualize the possibility of success.

"Get used to it!" Carla snapped back at him. "You're one of the brightest young men I've ever met! Discipline won't kill you. Carelessness will."

Rameck grinned at her again. "Do you know how little you are?" he said as he looked down at her, a smile on his face.

"I'm big enough to knock some sense into you!" she tossed back at him.

"Yeah, you're probably right," Rameck admitted. "I'm sorry, Carla. I'm gonna try harder."

"Scared of me, aren't you?" Carla teased him.

Rameck laughed out loud. "Not even a little bit. But I respect you a lot."

Carla always seemed to know exactly what the three young men from Newark needed on any given day. Sometimes she'd yell. Other times she'd tease. And many times she'd just offer honest encouragement when the going got rough.

In Carla's class later that week, a class called "Becoming a Master Student," the assignment was to write an acceptance speech for an award that they had received as doctors.

"What kind of award?" Sampson asked.

"Maybe you saved more lives than anyone else in your hospital, so they decide to give you an award. What would you say?"

"I'd just say, 'Aren't you glad you have me around here?'" Sampson said with a laugh.

"I expect more than that for this assignment," Carla said. "Your speech must be at least five minutes long, and it must include honest thoughts about your accomplishments and sincere appreciation."

When it was his time to get up, George, who didn't like to speak in front of groups, gave the best speech, the whole class agreed later. "I am very honored," he said, "to receive this award. But I do not take credit for my success alone. I could not have reached this goal if not for the help of all of you in this hospital, from the custodial staff to the secretaries on the floors, to the other doctors and nurses and medical professionals. Patient care here is a group effort, and all of us must share in the success of each of us. We work not for each other, but for our patients."

When he finished, the other students stood and applauded. "Save that speech!" Rameck yelled from the back of the room. "In fifteen years you may get to use it!" Everyone laughed, but George took the whole thing very seriously.

One day in Carla's class the conversation turned to personal appearance. "Doctors have to look like doctors," one student said. "They should wear dress pants and button-down shirts and always wear a tie."

"What do the rest of you think?" Carla asked.

"I think a doctor ought to look like a person," Sampson said. "I ain't changin' my style just because I'm going to school with a bunch of kids that roll around in money."

"You'd wear those baggy jeans and sweats to a hospital?" another student asked.

"Why not?" Sampson challenged. "What's wrong with them?"

"It looks ghetto," the student mumbled, afraid of Sampson's response.

"If I live in the hood, and I work in the hood, then my patients will think I'm dressed appropriately, don't you think?"

Sampson replied, a dangerous tone of anger in his voice. "After all, it is part of my culture and who I am."

"I think patients will respect us if we don't try to pretend to be something we never were. As long as we give good patient care, what difference does it make what we wear while we're doing it?" Rameck added.

"I think a patient might be glad to see we understand where he's comin' from and might be more likely to trust us than someone who comes in with designer pants and shoes," George said. "If I'm talking to a kid in my dental chair, and he's scared, he'll relax if I talk to him about rap music, or the latest shoes, or some issue from the streets. We've been there, so we know. It's all in how you handle it."

The rest of the class finally agreed, and the discussion helped to guide Rameck, George, and Sampson as they tried to make their place in the world of college and privilege. They decided early to be true to themselves first, so that they could be true to their patients later.

The seven weeks sped by quickly, and soon it was time for another graduation, this time to celebrate their entrance into college as preparation for medical school. George, Sampson, and Rameck now felt a lot more confident about facing the rigors of college work and thankful that their parents and teachers could once again applaud for them as they reached another milestone.

The keynote speaker that night was Dr. Francis Blackman, an African-American pulmonary specialist. "This Pre-Medical/Pre-Dental Plus program is an absolute necessity for our society," he said. "I applaud the young men and women who have completed this phase of the program, and I heartily encourage them to continue their studies as they plan to enter into medical fields."

George, Sam, and Rameck sat proudly as they listened.

"Our nation's health-care system is still a dual system, you know," Dr. Blackman continued. "African-Americans, other minorities, and all those classified as poor in this country still receive less than adequate treatment in facilities that are far outstripped by hospitals and clinics in wealthier neighborhoods."

Rameck nodded, knowing what the doctor said was true.

"Therefore, the life span for African-Americans and the others in the group is far shorter than their counterparts who can afford to pay for private care. America needs you, young doctors. The people who live in your communities need you desperately. I salute you for the journey you are about to undertake—not for yourselves, but for those children yet unborn who will live because you will be there for them."

Sampson felt a sense of pride as he welcomed the challenge. Rameck felt charged, excited, and ready to take on the world. All of them showed the same glow in their eyes—the look of the possibility of success on their faces.

THE POSSIBILITY OF SUCCESS

Seton Hall University opened my eyes to endless possibilities. It was there I learned the power of positive peer pressure. Instead of being surrounded by negativity, the three of us were engulfed by encouragement. We were thrilled to be around so many individuals who were making positive strides in their lives.

Carla and the rest of the staff believed in their students and pushed us beyond our own personal limits. I never knew I could study so much and take on so many tasks at once. Every day was a challenge, and I refused to fall short of the expectations of those around us.

When times were difficult, as they often were, Carla was there for us. She believed in our abilities long before we believed in ourselves. From the very first day, she called me Dr. Davis. Rameck she called Dr. Hunt, and George was always Dr. Jenkins. I thought that was pretty cool, and it helped us to see ourselves as doctors, because at first I was a little uncomfortable with the title. I guess that's because I didn't initially believe.

Young people need positive role models and guidance in their lives. There is no underestimating a positive figure in a child's life. I wish everyone could have a Carla Dickson in his or her corner. ▪

CHAPTER SEVENTEEN

"THE BOY'S NECK BENT IN AN ODD WAY, AND HIS BODY FELL LIMP."

FRESHMAN YEAR IN COLLEGE "Man, this is like living in another country!" Rameck said to George and Sampson as they crossed the green lawns of Seton Hall University early in their freshman year.

"Yeah, I feel you," George replied. Hundreds and hundreds of students—most of them white—seemed to surround them constantly. "I feel like a rock in a snowstorm—completely covered up."

"Some of the students are pretty cool," Sampson commented. "They smile, they're friendly, they even invite us to study groups. It's just that there's so many of them!"

"Yeah, man, it's hard to get used to," Rameck said with feeling. "I remember white salesclerks following me around stores—looking at me as if I was gonna steal something."

"And little old white ladies hugging their purses when I sat next to them on the bus or subway," George added.

"Or white police officers stopping me when I hadn't done anything," Sampson reflected. "It's just hard to get used to feeling normal around here."

"It's gonna take time," George commented. "I suppose they have to get used to us, too," he said with a chuckle.

The three of them shrugged and headed off to their various classes, which they loved. The preparation of the summer program had really helped, and they felt secure in their ability to do the academic work. The social aspect of living in the college atmosphere was a little more difficult, however.

One afternoon, Rameck and a couple of cousins who were visiting him got into a loud and silly argument in the dorm hallway. Students came out of their rooms, curious to see what the commotion was all about. Rameck, embarrassed by all the attention from a crowd of nosy students, reacted with anger instead of restraint.

"What y'all lookin' at? We just havin' a little disagreement. Go on back to where you came from!" Most of the students disappeared back into their dorm rooms, not wanting to antagonize Rameck any further. But two students remained.

"Didn't you hear what I said?" Rameck yelled in his loudest, most intimidating voice. "Get out of this hallway now!"

"I live here, too," one of the students replied, an arrogant smirk on his face. "You can't make me leave if I don't want to."

Rameck couldn't believe his ears. How dare this college boy challenge him in front of his cousins? "What did you say?"

Rameck asked the student in disbe-lief. Where Rameck came from, a challenge had to be answered. The result was never very pretty.

The young man, who looked completely unafraid of Rameck and his threats, repeated, "I'm not going anywhere. I have just as much right to be in the hallway as you do."

PERHAPS SHE SAW POTENTIAL IN RAMECK'S EYES. FOR REASONS HE WOULD NEVER KNOW, SHE GAVE HIM A SECOND CHANCE.

Even though he knew the student was right, Rameck felt his anger rise uncontrollably. He walked over to the boy and said, right in his face, "I'm counting to three. If you don't leave, you're gonna wish you had!"

The student laughed and said to his friend, "He's trying to threaten me! Ha! Like I care."

Rameck had reached the boiling point. "One," he said slowly and ominously. "Two," he continued, a harsh threat in his voice. "Three," he said finally. Rameck was pulsing with rage.

The bold and seemingly unafraid student did not budge. He just stared at Rameck with a confident look of challenge on his face.

Rameck, no longer able to control his anger, picked up the student, raised him over his head, then slammed him to the floor headfirst. The boy's neck bent in an odd way and his body fell limp.

Terrified, Rameck's anger dissipated. *Oh, my God, I've killed him!* he thought. Growing up, Rameck had been taught to fight when he was disrespected, to stand up for himself, even if it meant reacting violently. But Rameck knew he had crossed the line in this situation.

Then the boy moaned and moved on the floor. His friend helped him up and back to his room. The dorm hallway was completely empty now and eerily quiet.

Back in his room, Rameck prayed silently, repentant but unable to change what had happened. He waited, and at four A.M. the police knocked on his door and took him to an office on the first floor of the dorm. In his mind, he watched his scholarship and his dreams disappear. All his work and struggle to overcome obstacles would be gone like a wisp of wind through the trees.

In addition to the police, members of the administration, the student, and his mother sat in the room, all looking at Rameck with accusation and disgust. Rameck's heart sank.

"Is this the guy who assaulted you?" the officer asked the student.

"Yes, sir," the young man replied quietly. His arrogance had disappeared along with Rameck's anger.

"Do you wish to press charges?" the officer asked him and his mother.

The mother paused and peered at Rameck. He looked at the floor, ashamed, embarrassed, and angry at himself for losing control. Then she spoke. "No, officer, we don't want to press charges."

Rameck's head shot up in disbelief. "You don't?" he whispered.

The mother said nothing else. Perhaps she knew he would get kicked out of school. Perhaps she saw potential in

Rameck's eyes. But for reasons he would never know, she gave him a second chance.

Too shocked even to find the words to thank her, Rameck was allowed to return to his room. He still had to face a hearing of school officials, however, and amazingly, they, too, chose mercy and only put him on probation. What was even more surprising was that white students he barely knew came to his aid. One offered the help of his father, who was a lawyer; another offered to write a letter of support. Rameck was amazed and humbled, vowing never again to judge anyone just by race.

Rameck did his best to stay out of trouble for the next few months, yet he still felt restless and incomplete. "You know," he told Sampson and George one day, "of all of the dudes I used to hang out with in Plainfield, only three of us graduated from high school, and I'm the only one in college."

"Yeah, same with my friends—and it's not like they were dumb—the possibilities of making it just seemed so far away," George replied with a nod.

"I had never even seen a college campus until I got here," Sampson admitted. "It was like going to Mars—something completely out of reach and not even worth thinking about."

"We ought to do something about that!" Rameck answered with enthusiasm. "There are little dudes on the streets right now, just like we were, sittin' on some corner, about to get into trouble. Why can't we find them and show them the other side of the world?"

George and Sampson responded with excitement, the three of them trying to figure out a way they could reach out and help some kids and perhaps make a difference in their lives. "Let's form a club—no—an organization that reaches out to kids in the community!" Sampson suggested.

"What should we call it?" George asked.

"How about Ujima?" Rameck answered immediately. "*Ujima* in Swahili means 'collective work and responsibility to the community.' It's one of the seven principles of Kwanzaa."

"Perfect!" the other two agreed. Over the next few weeks, in between going to classes, studying for tests, and doing extensive work in lab classes, Rameck, George, and Sampson made the plans, found a faculty sponsor, and convinced the Student Government Association of the university to grant them permission to operate this new organization.

Of course, they had no money to work with, so they brainstormed ways to raise money quickly and easily and still have fun in the process.

"Let's throw a party!"

"Tight! We can call it Ujima Jam and invite kids from all the neighboring colleges," Rameck added.

The party was a rousing success. The music was loud, the DJ was cool, and the five-dollar admission fee from each partygoer added to the treasury of the newly founded help organization. It was the first of several such dances, which became favorite events on campus.

After they had enough money to work with, Rameck, George, and Sampson approached several elementary schools in Newark to try to arrange student field trips to the campus. It proved to be a bit more difficult than they had anticipated, because of liability and transportation issues, but they did end up working with a couple of schools from Brooklyn.

The kids came to the campus, wide-eyed and amazed. Ujima bought them lunch, took them on a tour of the campus, and answered their questions.

"Is college hard?" one little boy asked.

"It's no harder than high school," Rameck told him, "but there's a lot more work to do. If you study and do your homework, it's really pretty easy."

"Doesn't it cost a lot of money to go here?" a little girl wanted to know.

"Yes, it does," George told her. "But anybody who really wants to go to college can go. There are scholarships and loans and work programs available. You have to be willing to work hard and find the solutions to make it happen."

"You sleep here at night?" another child asked timidly.

"Yes, we live in a dormitory and only go home on the weekend, but lots of students live at home and come here every day on the bus or by car. You do what works best for you," Sampson explained. "But it's fun living here, because there are fewer distractions. It's easier, for me at least, to study here than at home."

One little boy, who had remained silent and looked bored, finally raised his hand.

"You have a question?" Rameck asked him.

"No, I just think all this is stupid. I don't need no college. I'm gonna get rich sellin' drugs!" He looked at Rameck, George, and Sampson defiantly.

The boy's friend, taking courage from his buddy, spoke up next. "And I don't need no college either. I'm gonna play for the NBA and make millions of dollars!" The rest of the students seemed to consider these two with admiration.

Rameck looked at them and smiled. "Well, me and my two friends here are gonna be doctors. And when some drug dealer shoots you," he said to the first boy, "or when you trip on the basketball court and break your leg," he said to the second boy, "and that's assuming the NBA decides to take your little short behind, we'll be standing there in the hospital, waiting to take care of you. We will be the ones getting paid, and you'll be forgotten leftovers."

The two boys scowled but said nothing. The other kids nodded with approval.

"You can have a future with meaning and respect and possibility," George added. "That's what college can do for you. Don't be afraid to dream beyond what you see on the streets every day."

THE END OF VIOLENCE AND
THE START OF GIVING BACK

I had to learn control. By no means did I want to forget where I came from or lose my culture; I just needed to modify my behavior. I had to learn to face a challenge without a violent reaction. Actually, that student was right, and I was very wrong. The situation had nothing to do with race—it was a learned reaction to the stimulus of a physical challenge. I was behaving the only way I knew how. I had never been exposed to anything else. I gradually learned to discipline myself so that I could deal with challenges with my mind instead of my fists. I will always be grateful to that student and his mother, who chose understanding instead of retribution. They gave me the chance to continue my dream.

Most of the kids I grew up with didn't dream big. People would tell me that college was hard, that it wasn't for people from our neighborhoods. It wasn't until I got to Seton Hall that I realized what they were saying was not true. The funny thing about it was that the people who were spreading that lie had never stepped foot on a college campus.

That's why it was important for us to figure out a way to expose the kids from our neighborhoods to college. So we came up with Ujima. The name fit perfectly; it meant collective work and responsibility, and that's what it really was all about—helping your neighbor. I learned the term from a book about the seven principles of Kwanzaa. That same book talked about the importance of catching our children while they are young, before they get a chance to go down the wrong road. Lots of people contributed to helping me; I felt very strongly that I needed to give back by helping the next generation. I still do. ■

CHAPTER EIGHTEEN

"YO, YO, YO! CHECK IT OUT! CHECK IT OUT!"

THE RAP YEARS "Man, we're good!" George said when the video was over. Rameck, George, and Sampson were looking at a video that had been made the day before, during a campus Fun Day. A video company called Fun Flicks had made video karaoke tapes for anyone who wanted to try. George, Rameck, and another rapper who called himself P.S. had recorded their own rap song.

"We could be professionals!" Rameck said.

"Don't get carried away," Sampson reminded them. "These rappers got money and agents and backing and all kinds of things we don't have. You're just some dudes who can put some words and beats together."

"What we gonna call ourselves?" George asked. "We ain't nothing but another rough tribe, trying to make it."

146

"That's it!" Rameck said with enthusiasm. "Another Rough Tribe—A.R.T. for short. That's what we'll call ourselves."

"So you're gonna give up on our dream to become doctors, drop everything to become rappers all of a sudden?" Sampson asked in disbelief. He shook his head. "Man, that's a hard road for people who chase that dream full-time."

"It's quick and easy money," Rameck reasoned.

"Is it easier than studying?" George asked.

"I tell you what," Sampson suggested. "We could do both, see which one jumps off first, and go with that one! But I think it's stupid to give up what we've got going here for the chance to become rap stars!" George and Rameck listened carefully as Sampson continued. "I mean, the thought is hot, but it's an uphill battle and a full-time commitment."

"That's cool," Rameck said with a grin as he jotted down more lyrics on a piece of notebook paper.

Rameck, George, and P.S. practiced their act whenever they could and even found a studio that gave them free practice time every once in a while. They had a cool-looking photo taken of themselves, wearing baggy jeans and hats flipped backward, to use for publicity and even managed to make a couple of demo tapes. Sampson chose not to rap with them, but he was there to offer advice and make hookups for the others.

"Hey, guess what?" Rameck announced with excitement one day. "I got us a hookup with Bad Boy Records. It's owned by Sean Puffy Combs."

"Man, that's big time!" George replied enthusiastically. "We got it made now!"

"That's definitely what's up," Sampson said.

George, Rameck, and P.S. headed to New York one afternoon and found the place. It wasn't a big studio, just an apartment complex in the middle of Harlem.

"Should we go up?" P.S. asked.

"We've come this far—we may as well," Rameck replied as they climbed the narrow steps.

When they found the correct apartment number, all they found was a couple of guys sitting around, looking unconcerned.

"What do you need?" one of them asked as he picked his tooth with a toothpick.

"Uh, we're rappers, and we want Puffy, uh, Mr. Combs, to listen to our demo tape," Rameck told him.

"He ain't here right now, but you can talk to the vice president of the company. He's in the bedroom." The young man pointed with his toothpick to the back room.

P.S., George, and Rameck entered the bedroom, where on the bed lay at least three hundred tapes just like theirs. They explained to the vice president that they were college students who wanted to be rappers, and they'd like for him to listen to their material.

"Yeah, man, that sounds cool. Put it here on the bed, and I'll listen to it this afternoon. I'll get right back to you," he promised.

They left, excited about the possibility of this new career, but weeks passed, and the phone call never came. They did, however, get several chances to perform their music in clubs.

One weekend they were booked to

THEY LEFT, EXCITED ABOUT THE POSSIBILITY OF THIS NEW CAREER. BUT THE PHONE CALL NEVER CAME.

perform as the opening act in a hip-hop club that attracted mostly college students.

"What's up, y'all?" Rameck shouted into the mike as they took the stage. "How y'all doin' out there? You ready to party? We're Another Rough Tribe, and we're ready to take you there!"

Cheers went up, the bass began pounding, and the crowd began to sway and dance to the beat of their words and rhythms. "Yo, yo, check it out! Check it out!" they yelled. "These beats are hot, man!" Another Rough Tribe was pulsing in the darkened room. The crowd loved their group, and they, in turn, loved the response. Their futures looked bright and full of music.

Because of the bright stage lights, all they could really see from the stage were rhythmic shadows as the crowd moved to their beats, but the sounds and the feeling were electrifying. Rameck, especially, was reminded of his days when he exulted in the audience applause back in high school. He inhaled the smoky glory and felt as if he could stay on that stage forever.

"When's your CD coming out?" someone asked when they had finished.

"Soon," Rameck promised, although he didn't have the slightest idea how they could accomplish that goal.

The months passed quickly. With Sam as a manager of sorts, George and Rameck performed when they could, went to classes when they had to, and dreamed of a very different future than medicine. But somehow the big hookup never materialized. They never did get that recording contract, but they did get to meet Sean Puffy Combs and Biggie Smalls, also known as

The Notorious B.I.G. A friend of theirs, the R and B singer Faith Evans, married Biggie Smalls, and occasionally they were invited to have dinner with them when the couple lived in New Jersey. George was always amazed at how much the three-hundred-pound Biggie Smalls could eat at one sitting.

Their on-again/off-again rap career took place during the tumultuous months of the East Coast–West Coast rivalry of Biggie Smalls and Tupac Shakur, who spoke eloquently of a world turned upside down. When each of them was gunned down in the next few months, it put a damper on the doctors' enthusiasm for rap. Besides, Sam, George, and Rameck had no means to keep trying to break out in the increasingly popular, and therefore more difficult, world of rap.

"We're outta money, man," Sampson said to Rameck one day when he brought up the subject of rapping again.

"He's right. We're out of cash, dude," George reminded him. "Besides, we've put in so much time here at school. We've only got another year before college graduation. College, man— think of it. I can count on one hand the dudes I know who graduated from college!"

"We've got a good act. I think we have a shot at success," Rameck insisted.

George sighed. "Look. If I stick this out, I *know* I can be a dentist. I have no guarantee I'll be a rap star or for how long. Groups are big one day and forgotten the next."

"Yeah, but . . ." Rameck began.

"You want to drop medical school for this?" Sampson asked him.

"Maybe," Rameck replied sullenly.

"I don't," Sampson said flatly. "We've come this far together, man. The three of us. We've got the chance to be doctors," he said, his voice showing dreamy emotion.

"You know what?" Rameck said finally. "You're right. Both of you. We're in this together. We're gonna be doctors." He sighed. "But it sure would have been a cool ride!" he added with a grin.

RAP STARS?

It was fun while it lasted, but we never seriously considered leaving all those years of preparation and study for the vague possibility of becoming rappers. I never really thought we had what it took to rap professionally. It seemed to me to be too much work for something that was uncertain at best. I'm not much of a gambler—I needed better odds. Continuing our medical studies seemed like a much more sensible risk.

Rap provided the soundtrack for our journey. Even today we can sit together and discuss what was going on in our lives by listening to old songs. The music motivated us and gave us a source of both strength and inspiration. It gave us a much-needed break from the academic intensity and was a creative outlet as well. I think it's really important that everyone have a hobby or outside interest. It makes you a stronger, more stable individual, and when your academic pursuits get difficult, you have something to break the tension and help you relax. Having an artistic outlet can sometimes lead to employment or at least a means to pull in some extra cash. In addition, creative outlets are good for the soul, as well as the community. Everyone benefits when art or music or literature is shared.

When it came time to make the decision about what to do with the rest of our lives, the three of us realized that although the music business was alluring and exciting, the dental and medical professions we had chosen were solid paths that would support us well for the rest of our lives. In the end, it was more an acceptance of reality than a change in direction of our lives. Music was the decoration. Medicine is the solid foundation. ■

CHAPTER NINETEEN

"FOR THE FIRST TIME SINCE HIGH SCHOOL, THE THREE OF US WON'T BE TOGETHER."

THE END OF COLLEGE "We got accepted into Access Med!" Sampson called out cheerfully to Rameck and George one sunny morning.

Access Med was a program that allowed premed college students to finish their senior year and take half of their first year of medical school classes at the same time.

"Cool!" said Rameck.

"I knew you two would get accepted," George said slowly. "Sampson, you're one of the few dudes who ever got an A-plus in organic chemistry. You've got a three-point-six grade-point average and are about to graduate cum laude."

"What can I say? Smarts just live here in this beautiful body!" Sam joked.

"And you, Rameck," George continued, "have a three-point-four GPA and better study skills than anybody I know."

"Well, maybe now we have a chance—a better chance—to survive that first year. I heard it's a killer," Rameck said quietly.

"Yeah, but we can handle it," Sampson told him.

"So how does this work?" Rameck asked.

"Hmm, let's see what all this paperwork says," Sampson replied. "We'll have to transfer to Rutgers for afternoon classes, while we take morning classes at Robert Wood Johnson Medical School."

"Sounds like a dream come true, but you know what that means, don't you?" George asked.

"Yeah, it means for the first time since high school, the three of us won't be together," Rameck replied, a serious look on his face.

"Well, we knew this would happen eventually," George said. "My plans all along were to go to dental school." George had been accepted at the University of Medicine and Dentistry in Newark. "I'm looking forward to it. But it's gonna be hard not having you two to hang with every day."

"Yeah, I know," Sampson said. "Don't worry, we are still going to be there for each other."

The three friends, who had seen each other through rough spots and failures, through successes and laughter and sorrow and close calls, would have to split up in order to reach their final dreams. Carla Dickson promised to be there for George and call him every week to encourage him.

Rameck and Sam packed up and moved out, but they stayed close to George, catching up with him almost every weekend at parties or playing a quick game of basketball and on some quiet evenings, when they just hung out and talked.

One night, after a particularly loud, serious party, the three of them sat together, talking about old times, laughing about teachers and classes, and relaxing in each other's company.

"You know," Sampson began, "I don't even know if I really even want to be a doctor. I mean, it seems cool and all, but I just don't know if it's for me."

The other two said very little but gave him the silent support he needed. "Why you feel like that?" George asked quietly.

"Remember that time we got the chance to watch that surgery and I bumped the surgeon while he was making the incision? I'll never forget how he screamed at me, yelling, 'What are you doing? You're in my way!'" Sampson sighed.

"Yeah, but that can happen to anyone if they've never been in an operating room before," Rameck told him.

"Well, I felt out of place and off balance. Even more, I wanted to give that surgeon something to think about for raising his voice at me. Maybe I should change my major to business. I'm awesome with numbers and calculations. Math comes so easy to me. I'd be a great entrepreneur!"

"You'd be an even better doctor," Rameck told him with authority.

Sampson continued, "Trust me, if not for our agreement to stick together, I would have switched majors a long time ago. Besides, four years of college, four years of medical school, and then residency is way too long. I need to get my career started. My family is dependent on my success, and they can't wait too much longer for me to make it."

"You know the grass always appears greener on the other side," George said. "I think you're in the place where you need to be."

Sampson continued. "Whatever. I talk to students all the time who say their lifelong dream was to be a doctor. That's not how it was for me. I just stumbled into this program, and now that I'm here, I'm not sure if that's what I really want."

"I get scared and unsure of myself, too, man," Rameck admitted.

"Yeah, but nobody seems to be as confused or frustrated as I feel most of the time," Sam said miserably. "This place is nothing like home. Everything on campus is so calm and perfect. As crazy as it sounds, I miss all the noise, the sirens from the police cars and ambulances, and the loud chatter outside my house at night. It is what I'm used to. I don't see anyone else around here struggling to get acclimated—they are used to this type of lifestyle."

"What we're doing isn't easy, but it's worth it," George said. We've gone too far to stop now," he added, trying to sound encouraging.

"Yeah, I know," Sam replied confidently.

"What makes this so different from Seton Hall?" Rameck asked. "You did really good while you were there."

"That was preparation, just classes designed to get us ready. This is the real thing, and the environment is different. The work isn't the difficult part. Sometimes it feels as if I am outta place here and invisible to everyone. Truly, it is like being on another planet. I know the administration has programs set up, but they don't always connect," Sampson admitted.

George, on the other hand, was really enjoying dental school. It was difficult not being with Sam and Rameck every day, but he loved his classes; and for the first time, he really worked diligently to study and master the material. For a while he lived at home, then in his mother's old apartment when she bought a house. He and his mother were very close, and he knew how hard she worked to make his dreams come true.

"I don't like you working all these hours, Ma," he told her when she took on a part-time job to help him pay his college tuition. "You be working fourteen-hour days and comin' home late at night. I worry about you, Ma," he said.

"I'm just fine. All you got to do to pay me back is become a dentist and make me proud."

"I feel guilty sometimes, Ma, you doing all this for me," he told her.

"When you have kids of your own, you'll understand," she said. "Now go study." She kissed him on his cheek and went into her own room.

Even the people in his old neighborhood seemed to be proud of him—at least most of them. Men would stop him on the street and ask him, "How's all that college stuff goin', boy?" George would nod and smile and give them a high five. Women sometimes fixed him meals, and even the kids looked up to the neighborhood boy who walked down the streets carrying thick books, well beyond their comprehension.

He relaxed, feeling comfortable on the streets that he ran as a kid, forgetting after four years at Seton Hall about dangers that lurked there.

One day, a bearded, scruffy-looking dude walked up to George and said, "Hey, man, you want to buy some speakers for your ride?" George, who had just bought an old car, thought that some new speakers would really make it rock.

"Yeah, man," George said casually. "What you want for 'em?"

"I got 'em 'round the corner. You can pay me what you think they're worth," the man said.

George drove the man to the place where the car speakers were supposed to be, but when they got to the location, a secluded spot near some woods, the man suddenly pulled out a gun.

Knowing he had forgotten the rules of caution on the streets, George felt like kicking himself. "I should have known better," he mumbled.

"You know what to do," the man said.

George grudgingly pulled out the last of his money—forty-five dollars—and the man ran away in triumph. George sighed and headed back home, glad the situation hadn't been any worse. He knew his car could have been jacked, or he could have just as easily been killed.

He went back to school, trying to balance dental school classes and responsibilities, friends and interruptions from the neighborhood, and his connections with Rameck and Sam as he struggled to maintain his grades and his sense of direction. It wasn't always easy.

Oh, no, George thought, *I've got Dr. Nicholas this semester!* George sighed as he looked at his class schedule at the beginning of his second year in dental school. Dr. Nicholas, known to be a difficult and demanding teacher, required each of his male students to wear a tie to class. George owned one tie, and he never wore it. He had never had occasion to learn to tie one. *What am I gonna do?* he thought.

He grabbed the tie, then rushed off to class. He got there a few minutes early and spotted a classmate. "Hey, man, can you help a brother out?" George asked, a little embarrassed, as he held the tie in his hand.

Instead of tying the tie for George, the student motioned for him to follow him to the bathroom. He showed George, step by step, how to knot the tie. Then he untied it and let George try. George practiced for a bit; then the two students looked at each other and smiled. From that moment on, the knot George wore was his own.

HANGING IN THERE

It takes a long time to become a doctor or dentist. After four years of college, when most students are completing their education with bachelor's degrees, medical and dental students immediately begin their studies in medical or dental school. That takes at least another four years, depending on the program. After that, doctors are required to do both an internship and residency at a selected hospital to complete their studies.

Sampson and Rameck got accepted into Access Med, a difficult program but worth the effort. It takes a lot of perseverance to hang tough with challenging choices. Our peers were making money, often illegally, while we struggled for every nickel to buy books and supplies. Our families, although supportive, could not possibly understand the pressures we lived with. It takes the support and understanding of close friends to make it through. Try to find someone with goals that are similar to yours, and use each other for strength and stability.

When Sampson and Rameck were in medical school and I was in dental school, it was rough not being together every single day, sharing classes and conversation and support. Inner doubts and fears were very normal—we all had them. Sometimes people try to suppress feelings of uncertainty and inadequacy, just to appear tough on the outside. I think it's much wiser to share those feelings and talk about them. It's amazing the help you can receive from supportive family and friends if you acknowledge your feelings. Because Sam was able to talk to us, we were able to walk with him through a difficult time. Each of us needed the others throughout this process. None of us would have made it without the other two. ▪

CHAPTER TWENTY

"DRIVING WHILE BLACK"

RAMECK, MEDICAL SCHOOL "That was a good fight, man," Rameck said to his friend Dax as they drove down the street early one rainy November morning. They had just watched the Mike Tyson–Evander Holyfield prizefight and were heading back to Rameck's place.

"Yeah, I can't believe Holyfield knocked Tyson out!"

"Took him eleven rounds!" Rameck replied with a laugh. "I bet tomorrow morning he won't even remember he was in a fight!"

Rameck drove carefully and within the speed limit, always aware of police cars, cruising the streets late at night, looking for criminals or likely suspects. While stopped at a red light, they saw three police cars parked at the corner. One of the officers looked directly at Rameck.

"Uh-oh, here it begins," Rameck said quietly to Dax. "Here come the boyz!"

The three police cars, lined up in single file, slowly began following Rameck's car.

"Why they sweatin' us, man?" Dax said. "We ain't done nothing wrong. Not one thing."

"It's not about being wrong. It's about being black," Rameck said, anger and regret in his voice.

"Why do they just assume we're up to no good?" Dax asked bleakly.

"Who knows?" Rameck answered as the three police cars followed their every turning and stop. "DWB—Driving While Black—is the newest crime, don't you know?" He looked in the rearview mirror, and none of the cars had on lights or sirens. They just followed, silent vultures in the darkness.

"Maybe you better stop," Dax suggested. "They have nothing on us. You're in medical school. I'm in law school. They're not gonna bother us."

Rameck sighed and pulled over slowly. At that moment, the last police car in the line pulled in front of Rameck's car, cutting him off. The officer in that car jumped out of his car, gun drawn.

The second officer turned on his floodlights and jumped out of his car as well, gun in his hand, ready to fire.

"You're going to jail, medical boy!"

"Get out of the car!" the policeman shouted.

Rameck looked at Dax, and they

stared at each other in fear. "They gonna kill us, man," Dax whispered.

Rameck slowly got out of his car, hands raised. "We didn't do anything, sir," he said.

"Shut up!" the officer snarled as he rushed over and slammed Rameck against his car. "Why didn't you stop?" the officer yelled in Rameck's ear as he frisked him.

"I did stop," Rameck said.

"Not soon enough!" the policeman screamed back.

"Why are you frisking me?" Rameck asked.

"Just shut up!" the officer yelled again. One of the other policemen began searching through Rameck's car.

"Hey, you can't go through my car like that!" Rameck said. "Why are you searching my car?"

The policemen ignored him and popped the trunk.

"You got any drugs or guns?" the policeman asked.

"Of course not. I'm a medical student, and my friend here is in law school."

"Aha! Look what I found!" one of the officers yelled gleefully from inside Rameck's car. He held up a small fishing knife, about the size of a pencil, which had been in the glove compartment.

"You're going to jail, medical boy!" the policeman said harshly. He snapped on a pair of handcuffs and left Rameck standing in the rain long enough to get soaked. Rameck, angry, embarrassed, and very afraid, was pushed into the back of the police car.

Dax was allowed to drive Rameck's car home, but Rameck was taken to the station and charged with interference with a police officer and possession of a deadly weapon. These charges were felonies, and if they remained on his record, he would never be allowed to be a doctor. All of his hard work and sacrifices, as well as the sacrifices of his family, would be forever destroyed.

Rameck was released the next morning, but he was upset and could not eat or sleep. It was so unfair. He couldn't believe, after getting so close, that all he had worked for was about to slip away.

"You ought to file a complaint, man," someone suggested. "That was a bogus arrest."

Rameck was hesitant, but he knew that he had to get the charges dropped. He found a lawyer.

"I'll help you out, son," the lawyer promised. "I'll see if we can get the charges dropped. I'll talk to the prosecutor and the arresting officer."

Rameck felt hopeful, but the lawyer called him back a few days later and told him the policeman refused to drop the charges because a complaint had been filed against him. Rameck reeled in despair.

All of Rameck's friends and fellow students in medical school were looking forward to graduation and accepting positions as interns in various hospitals. He couldn't do that. First he had to clear his name.

The trial date was set. Rameck's attorney did not show up. The judge set a new date. Again, Rameck's lawyer did not appear in court. A third trial date was set. And, unbelievably, Rameck's lawyer did not bother to come to the courthouse. The judge was livid.

"Listen, young man," the judge said, "your attorney has no

respect for you or your well-being. I'm going to set a new trial date, and this case will be tried with or without your lawyer. If I were you, I'd find a new one!"

Rameck nodded. Through a friendly doctor who had once treated his mother, Rameck found a new lawyer. Once again he showed up in court, wearing his suit, his tie, and his dreams.

"God, please help me out of this," Rameck prayed.

The trial began, but after a few moments, the prosecutors asked for a recess.

"What's the problem?" Rameck whispered to his new lawyer.

The lawyer went to speak to the judge and the prosecutors. He returned to Rameck with a smile on his face.

"They've lost the evidence!" he said triumphantly.

"You mean my little fishing knife?" For the first time in months, Rameck began to feel hopeful.

"Yes. They can't find it, so the judge has thrown the case out. You are free to go!"

Rameck whispered a prayer of thanks and hurried out of that courtroom forever. Now he could concentrate on his future.

THE POSSIBILITY OF
LOSING THE DREAM

Many people have said that I was always in trouble. Looking back, I think I would have to agree with them. But even when I wasn't looking for trouble, it seemed that trouble had no problem finding me. When I got stopped by the police and was arrested, I thought my life was over. All that I had worked for—all that the three of us had fought for together—was about to disappear. And for once, it wasn't my fault. I had done nothing wrong. That's what made the whole situation so frustrating. I could have thrown in the towel and given up, but I didn't. I had too much to lose.

Sure, it was hard to concentrate on school during that time, but deep down I knew I was going to be a doctor, and I had the faith that it was going to work itself out. I didn't have much faith in the system, but I believed in myself. That's what's necessary when hard times come—resilience. I know it's difficult to hold your head up high when you feel that by doing so, you'll get smacked around, but it's important to stand tall for what you know is right.

I think the reason I was still successful was because no matter what trouble I got into, I never gave up on my dreams. I always knew I was going to succeed. Throughout all the adversity, I triumphed when most would have given up. Everybody goes through difficult periods in life. The person who is successful is the one who doesn't quit. Failure was not an option for me. It never was and never will be. ▪

CHAPTER TWENTY-ONE

"SOMETIMES YOU GOTTA FAIL IN ORDER TO SUCCEED."

SAMPSON, MEDICAL SCHOOL Medical school was a different world. Their class was made up of 120 students. It seemed to Sampson that everyone had a family member or two who was a physician. That blew his mind.

One day in a microbiology class the professor instructed the students to place a specimen on the agar in order to see if bacteria would grow in the petri dish. *What?* thought Sampson. *What is he talking about? What is a petri dish? What is agar?* Sampson looked around the room, and everyone was following the professor's orders. He was the only one with a blank look on his face. The rest of the students had had lots of prior experience in medicine and laboratory work. Sampson felt increasingly confused and out of place as the weeks went by.

The gap that existed between him and the rest of his classmates was made very clear as Sampson boarded an elevator one day at the end of classes. A neurologist and urologist whom he had seen on campus many times were deep in conversation. Both of them ignored the young medical student who listened in.

"How was your weekend, Bob?" the urologist asked.

"Terrific, Artie," the neurologist replied. "I spent most of the weekend teaching my six-year-old niece how to use my stethoscope. She spent hours listening to her heart and everyone else's in the family as well. Then she moved on to listening to the humming of household appliances and insects!" He laughed. "She'll be a great doctor one day."

"Just like her uncle!" the urologist replied genially.

The two of them walked off the elevator, laughing and talking of other things. Sampson just stood there, overwhelmed by what he had finally figured out.

I was twenty-four years old the first time I picked up a stethoscope, he thought. *I had no idea what a heart or lungs might sound like when I listened through it.*

At six years old, Sampson had seen others use other instruments, like knives and guns, not ones that would make a difference in his life or the lives of others. Sampson couldn't help but envy the young girl. He had missed out on so much. Perhaps the road might have been easier if he had had some of those early opportunities.

He continued to have challenges, both in class and within himself. He knew that if he felt better about his place in this medical work, he would do better in school. But it was a vicious circle. Feeling out of place bred less-than-desirable efforts, which led to disappointing results. He felt himself spiraling downward.

He finally hit bottom when the letter came. Sampson slumped into a chair. His face wore a look of dejection and despair.

"What's wrong, man?" Rameck asked, although he had a pretty good idea of what Sam would tell him.

"I failed the state board medical exam," Sampson said in disbelief.

"Aw, dog, I'm so sorry," Rameck said. "But don't worry. It's gonna be all right. You get to take it again, man."

"Yeah, I know," Sam said. "Maybe this is a sign that I'm not meant to be a doctor."

"Don't talk crazy. This is just a temporary setback. How close were you to the pass point?"

"Three points," Sampson said with confusion. "I studied hard, man. Shoot, we studied together, staying up all night, cramming for this one test that determines everything."

"I know you knew the material," Rameck said gently. "You had it down cold."

"Yeah, I know. Well, it all left me. My brain was a blank, and I shut down the day of the test. I just couldn't think. It wasn't the test itself—I knew the material. It was my lack of focus, I guess."

"It's no big deal. You get to take it again," Rameck said with encouragement.

Sampson shook his head. "It *is* a big deal. I've told you before—I'm torn about this doctor stuff. I don't know any doctors, I didn't grow up around doctors, and I don't have any doctor friends. And it isn't as if the medical school is trying to help a kid from the ghetto get it together. They can't relate to the struggles and hardships I've been through."

Rameck touched Sam's shoulder. "I can, man."

"I'm not looking for any sympathy or pity. I'm just looking for my angle and place in medicine where it all makes sense. I was prepared for the test, man, but I just psyched myself out, that's all."

"All of us feel like that at one time or another," Rameck told him. "We're in this together, remember?"

"Yeah, but we didn't fail this exam together. I'm in this one by myself," Sam reminded him.

Every morning, instead of going to the hospital with the rest of the medical students, Sampson went to the medical library. He went over biology, microbiology, anatomy, and physiology. He quizzed himself and pushed himself, determined to pass the test with a high score when he took it again.

He spent time with Carla Dickson and challenged himself to find his place in medicine. He played basketball and exercised regularly to help clear his mind and reduce stress. There were plenty of quiet times, when he would pray to God, asking for strength and direction. He knew he would find answers to his dilemma.

When the time came to retake the exam, Sampson felt much more relaxed and confident. He knew the material, and the answers came quickly. When it was over, he knew he had passed with flying colors. He breathed a deep sigh of relief and sent up a silent prayer, "Thank you, God."

When the official letter came to verify that Sam had indeed passed the test, he and George and Rameck went out to celebrate.

"I knew you'd ace it, man," George told him as they stuffed themselves with cheesy pizza.

"Yeah," Sampson admitted. "I needed that to happen. There was a reason for it, and I know sometimes you gotta fail in order to succeed."

"You got the right stuff," Rameck told him with sincerity. "You're gonna be a dynamite doctor."

"Yeah, you're right," Sampson agreed. "We are going to be great doctors."

The next two years passed quickly, with Sampson and Rameck taking clinical rotations at various hospitals in pediatrics, surgery, family practice, obstetrics, and other fields. The purpose was for students to learn by observation and sometimes participation in the care of patients in different departments of the hospital. George did the same in the dental clinics. Sampson easily passed the next board exam that came up, and he maintained high grades throughout the rest of medical school.

As they got closer to graduation, each medical student was to decide what field he or she wanted to specialize in and then apply to various hospitals for job placement. The hospitals sorted through the applicants and accepted those they wanted. Computers matched young doctors and positions from all over the country. The anticipation built up to extreme tension and excitement. It was a little like the NBA draft, and it was the most important day in the senior year of medical school. It was called Match Day, and every single medical student in the country opened his or her letter at the same time.

Rameck decided he liked internal medicine, while Sampson felt really comfortable in emergency medicine. He liked the fast pace and variety of that department, where cases could vary from gunshot wounds to dog bites to upset stomachs.

But he had waited until the last minute to file his paperwork, and no slots in emergency medicine seemed to be open. Faced with limited options, he applied for a position in internal medicine, but his heart was not in it.

On Match Day, Rameck gleefully opened his letter, which confirmed his position in internal medicine at Robert Wood Johnson Medical School in New Brunswick. Sampson didn't bother to open his letter at first, because he knew it offered a position in an area of medicine he did not want to pursue.

Later, however, Sampson signed the letter of intent that promised him a slot in internal medicine at the University of Maryland. Glumly he went through the motions of finishing school. He felt despondent, unable to maintain any excitement about his future. He felt lost, in limbo. Finally, he called Carla Dickson. Carla was always there for him, as well as Rameck and George.

"I can't do this," Sampson told her. "I can't spend the next year doing something I hate. I'd rather quit."

"You're not a quitter, Sam," she told him. "What is it you really want to do?"

"Emergency medicine. But there were no matches, no openings." He sighed.

"Follow your heart and pray, Sampson. The answer will come to you," Carla told him with confidence.

"Why bother? It's too late now anyway," he said.

"It's never too late. You can't walk around in a pit for the next year. Go for it!"

Sampson, feeling hopeless, but somehow having too much persistence and determination to give up, suddenly had an inspiration. *Maybe I'll just check the Internet and see what's out there*, he thought. For some reason, he felt a glimmer of possibility, almost as if this idea had been divinely inspired.

He sat down at the computer and typed in RESIDENCY IN EMERGENCY MEDICINE. The computer whirred for a minute; then the name NEWARK BETH ISRAEL HOSPITAL appeared, with a contact number. The computer page said all the positions were filled.

This couldn't be possible. How could Newark have a program and I didn't know about it? No harm in calling, Sampson said to himself. *But since I'm from Newark, maybe they can find a place for me.*

He knew this was a long shot. Early in the matching process Sampson had filled out the electronic form for emergency medicine, and over 100 training programs were listed.

Newark Beth Israel, however, had not appeared on that original list.

He picked up the phone and made the call. "Hello. This is Newark Beth Israel Hospital. I'm Jacquie Johnson, Resident Coordinator. How may I help you?"

"My name is Sampson Davis. I'm a graduate of the University of Medicine and Dentistry of New Jersey—Robert Wood Johnson Medical School, and I did not match in emergency medicine. I just discovered that you have a residency at Beth Israel, and I would desperately love to become associated with you if you have any openings." He explained the whole story to her.

"You know, Dr. Davis, your life must be guided by divine intervention," she said. "Just yesterday we had a cancellation in emergency medicine. We have an opening! Fax me your information right away."

Overjoyed, Sampson sent the information, then waited for the phone call that would determine his future.

The phone rang. "Hello, Dr. Davis, this is Jacquie at Beth Israel. The program director is very interested in talking to you. Can you come for an interview on Wednesday?"

When Sampson walked through those hospital doors, he knew right away that Newark Beth Israel was the place for him. The smells of antiseptic and astringent seemed to energize him, and the feelings generated by human trauma and fear seemed to motivate him. He answered the interview questions with ease and confidence and was offered a position just two days later. It was as if his prayers had been answered. Somehow, he had snatched victory from the jaws of defeat. His life was summed up by this one experience.

He would be returning as a doctor to the same hospital where he was born, the same hospital where he was taken when the rock crushed his foot, the same hospital where the seeds of his interest in medicine had first been planted. Dr. Sampson Davis was going home.

A CONVERSATION WITH
DOCTOR SAMPSON DAVIS

GOING BACK
TO WHERE IT ALL BEGAN

Impossible! I went all over the country, interviewing at different facilities, while all the time my place was right back at home, where it all started. I couldn't have scripted it better. To be back home taking care of individuals I went to school with and neighbors, friends, relatives, and people from the community was simply priceless. That experience made me believe that some things are out of our control, and only faith can see us through. When times get hard, as they certainly will, and the situation seems hopeless, as it certainly will seem to be at times, spiritual belief and old-fashioned faith are powerful allies to see you through.

When it looked as though I would have to take a job in internal medicine, it seemed as if my struggles had been meaningless. Just at the point when I was finally supposed to capture success, it was going to be snatched away from me. But with faith, a little good fortune, and my 3 D's—discipline, determination, and dedication—I was placed at the hospital where it all began. The same hospital where I was taken for my broken foot so many years ago became the place where I began my practice of medicine. From a frightened six-year-old patient to a confident twenty-six-year-old doctor. Who would have believed it could be possible? ■

CHAPTER TWENTY-TWO

"TO FRIENDS"

GRADUATION FROM MEDICAL SCHOOL It was May 26, 1999, a beautiful sunny morning. Graduation day. Not from elementary school, or high school, or even college. This was the day that Sampson, Rameck, and George would graduate from medical and dental schools. Eight long, hard years had passed since they left University High School and headed off to Seton Hall, unsure and unaware of where life would take them. They had undergone personal trauma, self-doubt, and potentially disastrous situations. Much personal sacrifice, as well as the sacrifice of family members who had encouraged and supported them along the way, had made it possible. They had run out of money, out of food, out of hope at times. They had studied, laughed, partied, played, and studied some more. Each of them had almost lost his way many times, then found it again, thanks to the help of the other two when the need arose. They had survived—and succeeded.

Amazingly, the ceremonies for all the New Jersey Schools of Dentistry and Medicine were held at the same time and at the same place, so the three doctors could be together for this landmark moment as well.

Slowly, in alphabetical order, according to the various school or discipline, the names of the candidates for graduation were called.

"Doctor Sampson Davis." Sam strode across the stage, black gown and colorful hood flowing behind him. His family, as well as Rameck and George and their families, cheered wildly as he accepted his diploma. Sam thought back to the three skinny boys in tennis shoes who had once made a pact to stick together and make something of themselves.

"Doctor Rameck Hunt." Rameck, his dimpled grin pasted broadly across his face, stood and accepted his degree. He thought of hard times and critical situations and of friends who never had the chance to make it to this place.

"Doctor George Jenkins," the voice called out as the candidates for the School of Dentistry were called. George wanted to laugh out loud. This was the day he had strived for, had secretly desired all his life.

Sampson, the man with determination and drive. George, the man with the long-range vision. Rameck, the questioner, the activist, the cheerful encourager. The three friends, who had grown from awkward, confused teenagers to men proudly walking across a stage to accept medical degrees, had brought each other through. It was a moment of well-deserved glory.

Days later, after all the congratulations had been offered, the bags had been packed, and their lives were beginning a new phase, the three doctors met for relaxation and drinks. Each knew what the other had been through. Individually, their roads had held impossible obstacles. But together, their combined strength had taken them through to success. They had beaten the streets.

"To friends," said Sam.

"To friends," Rameck repeated.

"To friends," George added. They clinked their glasses together in a triumphant toast. There was nothing better that could be said.

SOMETIMES FACT IS MORE AMAZING THAN FICTION. Our lives attest to that truth. We managed to survive temptation, incarceration, and distraction. We were faced with a lack of money, lack of knowledge, and occasionally a lack of confidence in our ability to succeed. But we managed, through patience, perseverance, and positive thinking, to grow from scrawny teenagers with doubtful futures to become medical professionals highly respected in our community. Individually, we probably would have failed. Together, we made it through.

We have tried to offer you insights and inspiration so that you, too, can find hope and a dream of success. We learned, sometimes the hard way, that self-control is essential and that peaceful solutions are always preferable to violent ones. Even though it was difficult, we discovered that we had to resist all the negative peer pressure around us. We easily could have drowned in that sea of despair.

What other messages can we leave with you? Find people who inspire and encourage you and stick with them. Pick your friends carefully—those with goals similar to yours. But remember, one good friend is better than dozens of fake people who won't have your back in time of trouble. Be careful of giving in to negative peer pressure. Please yourself, and you'll never be disappointed.

Depend on your friends for strength and support, and be sure to communicate with them openly. Don't be afraid to have doubts and fears. It's normal to have them and healthy to talk about them. Try to have the same goals and ideals as the people you hang with, and compete in a healthy way. Jealousy of another's success is a sign of weakness, not of a strong friendship.

Don't be afraid to stand up for what's right—be a leader instead of a follower because aimlessness is dangerous. Set goals for yourself, and no matter how impossible they may seem, never give up. The person who is successful is one who doesn't quit.

When you see trouble going down, remove yourself from the situation. When you're making a decision, consider the consequences. Smart choices will keep you in the game. And if you falter or make mistakes, remember that everybody has stumbled. Pick yourself up and move on. Never give up on yourself. Some things are out of your control, and a strong dose of faith might be the only thing to see you through.

Don't be afraid to dream big. Dream yourself successful. No one aims to become a failure. When you are given the chance to succeed, it is your responsibility to make the most of it. Have faith in yourself and your future.

These words may sound familiar—the same words that adults toss at you all the time—but remember that we lived through unbelievably terrible situations, and these words have real meaning in our lives. We feel that our purpose in life is to offer you a beacon of light, a path to follow. We've been where you are, and we want to help you avoid the rocks on the path we took. Remember, the brighter your future is, the brighter everyone's will be.

Finally, it is extremely important to give back to your community, to your roots, to those who helped you. It is your way of giving thanks for the successes—to offer inspiration and motivation to those who follow you or look up to you. That's why we started The Three Doctors Foundation. Our mission is to inspire and create opportunities for communities across America. Our focus is Health, Education, Leadership, and Mentoring.

WHAT ARE WE DOING TODAY? Drs. Rameck Hunt and Sampson Davis graduated from the University of Medicine and Dentistry of New Jersey—Robert Wood Johnson Medical School. Dr. George Jenkins graduated from the University of Medicine and Dentistry of New Jersey Dental School. Dr. Sampson Davis was for many years an emergency-medicine physician at the same hospital where he was born in Newark, New Jersey. Now he is a board-certified emergency-medicine physician at East Orange General Hospital and St. Michael's Medical Center, and a consultant for the Violence Prevention Institute focusing on gang awareness and preventive medicine in Essex County, New Jersey. Dr. George Jenkins is a professor at the University of Medicine and Dentistry of New Jersey, and Dr. Rameck Hunt is a professor and director of the outpatient clinic at St. Peter's University Hospital in New Brunswick, New Jersey.

In addition to our heavy medical schedules, we do lots of traveling to support youth in communities around the country. The Three Doctors Foundation offers a series of positive community activities including health fairs, leadership presentations, holiday outreach programs, and mentoring sessions for teen and preteen youth. For more information, please visit us on the Web at www.threedoctors.com

Our thanks go to Sharon M. Draper, author of several very successful books for teenagers, who brought our biographies to life. She took the essence of our life stories and made them palatable and enjoyable for a youth and teen audience. We met with her here in New York, and the four of us really "clicked." If you'd like to contact her or learn more about her, go to her Web site at www.sharondraper.com.

We hope you share this book with others, use it as a tool for inspiration and motivation, and make all your dreams come true. We believe in you!

Sincerely,
The Three Doctors

183

SHOUT-OUTS!

The story of our lives and friendship is in many ways also the story of our families and friends. We'd like to thank them for the courage they displayed throughout this project and the trust they placed in us as we shared the good and the bad. Much of this book is about the positive influences that people along the way had on us, yet there were times when some members of our families and friends were victims of circumstances that didn't allow them to be there for us, and some even caused us pain—either knowingly or unknowingly. It is possible that if we hadn't faced those difficulties, we wouldn't have had the conviction and motivation to make it to where we are today, or the empathy for others that our experiences afforded us. We are truly grateful and feel tremendously blessed by the love and generosity that our families have demonstrated toward us. Our individual thanks are listed below. But first, the three of us collectively would like to thank the great many individuals and institutions that helped to transform each of our lives. Among them are: our classmates, and the teachers, advisers, and other staff who supported us at University High School, Seton Hall University, the Robert Wood Johnson Medical School, and the University of Medicine and Dentistry of New Jersey in Newark. We are forever indebted to Carla Dickson, who was surely sent by God to guide us through. We give thanks to Dr. Linda Hsu for standing by us during college, medical, and dental school. We owe much of our success to the Pre-Medical/Pre-Dental Plus Program and Access Med, two affirmative-action programs that simply gave us a chance. If we had lived in other states where such programs have come under attack, we probably would not have been afforded the opportunities that helped to make us who we are.

We are grateful to Joann Davis for helping us to embrace the book world, to Lisa Frazier Page for her extraordinary work on *The Pact*, and to our editor Stephanie Owens Lurie and Dutton Children's Books for the opportunity to make our story accessible to even younger audiences.

To Dr. Noble and Mrs. Mann, thanks for realizing before anyone else— even us—that we had a story to tell. To all who helped us convey our message of hope, we say thanks, particularly:

To Caryl Lucas, who wrote the first *Star-Ledger* article, which turned into many more; Kaylyn Dines, who stayed behind us and made things happen; Windy Smith, for all your work with the Three Doctors Foundation; Kim Holiday, for all your work with the Web site development; Susan Taylor, Ed Lewis, and Clarence Smith, for introducing us to the world.

FROM GEORGE JENKINS:

This effort is dedicated to the people and things that make me who I am, and why:

1. My people, for always believing in me and never doing anything but support and nurture my aspirations.

2. My city, specifically the Central Ward. Living here fills me with so much purpose and determination for change that I can't even begin to help you understand if you don't already.

3. My circle, for all you do: Garland, Sam, Rameck, Shahid, Na-im, Tone Webb, Roz, Faye, Orlando, Ant Brown, and Al Brown.

4. My classmates, UHS Class of '91 and NJDS Class of '99, especially Rhoda Pruitt, Alicia Grey, Cathleen Woods, and Denise Davis, for all the lessons we learned together.

5. My other father, Shahid Jackson, Sr., for being there. You always

believed in me. I believe in you, too, as you make your dreams come true.

6. My block, for keeping it real: Reggie and Kenny, Lace, Tiffy, Steffy and Kenyor, Mandy, Bruce and Gett, Hak and Fuquan, Smiley, Marv, Samad, Brian Jackson, Usef, Sneaky Pete, Shoronda and Malika, Sockie and Vonetta, Lebrashaun and family, Rahman and Abdul, Denaaman, Sherri and the Washingtons, the Seaburns, Farad (Hold your head up. I'm riding with you) and the Greens, Anwar, Toy and little Puff (I see you winning computers and things for an essay on me at school. Keep it up), Rasheed Jackson, Brian, the counselor at the Central Ward Boys' Club (Thanks for being something different from what was all around me at the time), Chuck and Wop (Thanks for starting elementary school with me and, despite whatever changes you had to face, always encouraging me to keep it moving). When your community encourages you rather than tears you down, great things can come from nothing at all. RIP—Anton, Duane, Brian McKoy, Wayne Smiley, and Ms. Willie Mae.

7. My mom, for all you did—and still do—for me. Because you had the drive to get your son's crooked teeth fixed for his future, you inadvertently provided one of the biggest inspirations for his future. You have always tirelessly given so much of yourself to make sure I was on point or could concentrate on school as much as possible, and you are the root of my inspiration, whether you realize it or not. Just know that I love you for all your dedication and that I will always have your back the way you had mine, Ma Dukes. I deeply appreciate you with all my heart even when I am not showing it, please believe it.

FROM SAMPSON DAVIS:

To my mother: after God comes you. Thank you for not giving up and running out on us. You are by far the strongest person I have ever known. I love you with all that I have. Realize that faith can overcome all. You taught me to put God first and the rest will follow.

To my father, thank you for being there for me. You taught me how to be a man. Your dedication and dignity taught me how to stand tall and face my responsibilities in good and bad times.

To my brothers and sisters, Kenny, Rose, Fell, Andre, and Carlton, I shared our lives in an attempt to help others. I love you guys and thank you for standing by me.

To all of my family, cousins, aunts, uncles, nieces, and nephews—thank you for embracing my efforts and message. This journey is forever elevating and showing itself in different forms.

To all of my mentors—Carla, Dr. Hsu, Reggie, Dr. Essien, Mom, Pop, countless teachers and doctors—you are the educators. When I speak to kids about their future and to adults about their health, there is nothing more rewarding than when I know I have made a difference. And believe me, you all have made a difference in my life.

To the city of Newark and all our communities—we did it. My work is for the kids who wish to achieve, for the adults who still believe. It can be done. There have been people in my life who told me that I couldn't do this. To them, I give thanks—because they are the ones who made me dig deeper than I even imagined and reach heights that I once thought were unattainable.

To my sister Fellease, I miss your laugh, your stories, and your smile. You taught me how to live life for the moment, how to make the most out of every situation. Thank you for believing in me. You were always my bullhorn, making sure everyone knew I was your brother, The Doctor. I miss you, Sis, and will see you on the other side. Love ya.

To my niece Vanessa—I am so proud of you. Keep pushing forward. Congratulations on your acceptance to Montclair State University

To Sabu, Camille, Will, Dax, Altareek, Serron, Nyjgel, Rabu, Al, Nnamdi, Patrick, Maria, Derrick, Gerry, Diab, Karma, Paul, Noody—many laughs, many great times, we truly live it to love it. All about the moment, it is so necessary.

To Mary, Carole, Frankie, Francina, and Alex—thank you for opening your home to me. It's funny how three months became years.

To the Emergency Department at Beth—you guys make it fun. Keep making your mark on the medical world.

To Windy—you have helped to propel the Three Doctors to new heights. I know it is tough at times dealing with the demands on our schedules, but you never break a sweat. You are a gem. Thanks, Sis, for all your hard work and dedication.

To all of the Three Doctors Foundation volunteers—you all amaze me. None of you ever miss a beat. You are at every function, Saturday morning, bright and early. Your effort emulates what the Three Doctors are all about. Thank you for your commitment to the community and for continuously giving back.

To Darrell—thanks for sharing the vision. It is always a win-win situation.

To Julian Riley—thanks for all of your legal advice and your friendship. Your guidance is on point and in line with our progress.

To Congressman Chaka Fattah, thank you for embracing our mission. Your goal is our goal, higher education for all. Continue the great work.

To all of the Three Doctors sponsors and supporters, thank you and please continue to support our projects. We are the faces for health and education, the LeBron James of medicine and education. We will continue our efforts in making health, education, leadership, and mentoring more commercial, savvy, and acceptable to the public. We will continue to place projects that speak to society's needs in an effort to help promote the more positive goals in life and to deliver a blueprint for individuals to follow. We want all of our communities, regardless of background and location, to be successful and to realize there is power in numbers. I encourage all readers to go out there and form a pact. It is extremely important to have someone to simply lend a nonjudgmental ear in time of need. We all are the future, we must continue to push forward and never give up regardless of how tough times may get. Continue on and continue to embrace our mission, the Three Doctors are forever.

For those whose names I didn't mention, know that you, too, are a part of my success, and I thank you.

I must single out my boys, Gee and Rah. Man, we have done it all! We couldn't have planned this outcome, even if we tried. It is amazing what can happen through friendship and education. Our road traveled was a blind venture. Many times we tripped over our own shoelaces. But we never stop believing in one another. We have so many countless memories and so many more to come. Thank you for the ride. There is nothing the three of us can't accomplish. We are the beacons of hope for so many.

FROM RAMECK HUNT:

First and foremost, I'd like to thank God. Truly, God deserves all the credit and praise, because without Him, there would be no us. God took three young boys and made them into men. Through us He is showing the world what miracles are made of and is spreading a message—a message of perseverance, true friendship, love, dedication, and trust. He teaches us the lesson of caring and giving back—each one teach one. Only God could produce the miracle that we are, and to Him I am forever thankful.

I am so thankful that I have friends and family to share my life and my love. I feel really loved, and I thank you all and love you so much, especially:

My mother, for instilling values in me early on. Without them I don't know if I would have made it. Even though we had our share of problems through the years, what you taught me will last a lifetime. I love you so much, Mom.

My father, for listening to me when I needed you. Just watching you and listening to you reminds me that I came from your seed. We are so much alike, and I am proud and thankful that I inherited such wonderful genes. Love you, Dad. Thank you for all the lessons you taught me.

My late grandmother, Ellen Bradley. I love you and I know you are my angel, watching over me.

My sisters, Daaimah, Mecca, and Quamara. I love all of you and I would do anything in this world for you. Thank you for loving me. You may not know it, but just checking up on me from time to time meant so much to me.

My aunts and uncles, Rasheed, Sheldon, Gloria, Nicole, Victoria, Venus, Rahman, Teresa, Kenny, and the late Anthony and Jackie, I love you all. Thanks for being there for me.

My cousins, thanks for keeping me humble. I'm still Mr. Potato Head.

My friends. I learned a lot from all of you, bad and good, lessons that I will take with me always, lessons that made me who I am. I'm so glad to see that so many of you, like me, have changed your lives and are doing the right things.

The love of my life, continue to stand by me and hold me down like you do.

And Nana. You showed me the importance of family (and Sunday dinner).

The brothers I never had: Sam and George. We have been through a lot together and will go through so much more. But I want both of you to know how much I appreciate your friendship. "I am my brother's keeper," as I'm sure you are mine.

FROM SHARON M. DRAPER:

Thanks, as always, to my husband, Larry, who is the only one who really understands the "process."

To Crystal, Damon, Cory, and Wendy—my first and best audience.

For Mary and Zelda, who are so good for Damon and Cory.

For Jasmine and Landon—my Florida sunshine babies.

For Elijah, Malachi, and Deshawn—my Minnesota snowmen.

For Vicky and Jeffery—remember the ice cream man and lightning bugs?

And of course, thanks always to Mom and Dad, who gave me wings to fly.

HERE'S WHAT YOUNG-ADULT READERS HAVE WRITTEN TO SAMPSON, RAMECK, AND GEORGE ABOUT THEIR FIRST BOOK,

THE PACT:

"I just finished reading your book and I was just speechless the way God can work in people's lives and how focused you were. The book was very inspirational and an eye-opener to me. The book has inspired me to set a better example to my peers and my little brother to show it is okay to be smart, to have big dreams, and to read all the time. I do these things but have not tried to influence others. The part of the book that really touched me was when you failed the board exam and you bounced back."

—HIGH SCHOOL STUDENT FROM AKRON, OHIO

"After reading your book, my negative and defeative [sic] attitude has gone out the window, and I will not accept failure by any means. I have dedicated myself to getting my GPA up to a standard where I can get into law school and help people—maybe not criminal law but labor law. Thank you for showing me that times get rough but success can still be achieved. Keep on doin' what you're doin'."

—COLLEGE STUDENT

"I was fortunate enough to finally finish your book. My mother made me read it and I am so pleased that I did. It made a huge impact on my life. It really taught me what it's like on the streets

and how you had to be your own role models. Living up to your expectation must be an honor. You've made a huge impact on many men and I hope I can someday be remembered just like you guys. I would have never known about this book if my mom hadn't got it and said, "READ, READ, READ." And I am very proud to have a mom like yours who didn't allow me to lose my life."

—Teenager from Essex County, New Jersey

"I recently graduated from high school. My graduation gift was your book *The Pact* and I enjoyed it tremendously. As a kid growing up in Kingston, Jamaica, a successful future was unheard of. Reading your book has made me more determined to become a lawyer, and I want to thank the three of you for giving me more inspiration when I needed it the most. Thank you!"

—Teenager from East Hartford, Connecticut

"I wrote to you about how your book has really inspired me. I am now majoring in biological sciences. I hope to finish in four or five years so that I could go to med school. I hope you are doing well. I just want to say thank you. I had doubts about having a career in medicine but after reading your book, I felt better and I hope to do well for the next few years."

—College student from New Jersey

Visit *www.threedoctorsfoundation.org* or *www.threedoctors.com* and share your thoughts about We Beat the Street with the Three Doctors.

For more information, visit www.pactpowerkids.com.